T5-CRP-192

Cloud Days
and Fire Nights

Cloud Days and Fire Nights

Canticles for a Pilgrimage Out of Exile

Edward F. Gabriele

Foreword by Edward F. Gabriele
and Stephanie R. Gray

Saint Mary's Press
Christian Brothers Publications
Winona, Minnesota

Genuine recycled paper with 10% post-consumer waste.
Printed with soy-based ink.

The scriptural passages in this book are freely adapted. These adaptations are not
to be understood or used as official translations of the Bible.

The publishing team included Carl Koch, development editor; Mary Duerson,
copy editor; Lynn Dahdal, production editor and typesetter; Maurine R. Twait
and Kent Linder, cover designers; PhotoDisc, Inc, cover photograph; Michael
O'Neill McGrath, illustrator; Maurine R. Twait, art director; pre-press, printing,
and binding by the graphics division of Saint Mary's Press.

The illustration of the sun used throughout this book is from *Clip Art for Year B,* by
Steve Erspamer (Chicago: Liturgy Training Publications, 1993). Copyright © 1993
by Archdiocese of Chicago. Used by permission of Liturgy Training Publications.

Copyright © 1997 by Saint Mary's Press, 702 Terrace Heights, Winona, MN 55987-
1320. All rights reserved. No part of this text may be reproduced by any means
without the written permission of the publisher.

Printed in the United States of America

Printing: 9 8 7 6 5 4 3 2 1

Year: 2005 04 03 02 01 00 99 98 97

ISBN 0-88489-426-6

For Stephen, Paul, and Richard
now that the hurricane has passed
and the first terrors of our exile
have given way to the ecstatic Grace of Freedom.

In thanks for all our friends
who helped strengthen our feet
to leave the fleshpots and enter Freedom's Desert
to wonder and to wander in delight
at the avenues of life's new possibilities
that God was opening before us.

To these my classmates and loyal friends,
and to every exile forced to wander
at the hands of human hatred, ignorance, and fear,
this volume of prayer is lovingly dedicated
in the hope of that Final Day of Peace
when every one of us shall be welcomed
Home.

Contents

Part D

Part E

Foreword

From the roots of the Judeo-Christian tradition, believers of every age have been stretched by a God who always seems to be present to us in ways far beyond the limits of our expectations. The God of the Scriptures indeed is a God of surprises unbounded by narrow human perceptions of what we think should or should not be deemed as "holy and acceptable."

Throughout our spiritual history, stories of faith recount again and again how the presence of God is made visible to us in persons and situations that some people in our world would not judge as fitting vessels for the message of grace. Yet even within the Scriptures, our greatest ancestors in the faith were hardly the perfect or mainstream characters of their times. Abraham and Sarah, Moses and Aaron, Judith and the prophets, Mary and Joseph, Peter and Paul— these individuals, as we can see if we scratch beneath the whitewash of their popular images, were real human beings living in ways that would have raised some eyebrows among their own circles.

Even Jesus is portrayed as having a lifestyle that was not mainstream for his time and was the cause of strong reaction, confusion, and gossip. Sometimes the most dramatic and enduring in-breakings of grace in history come to us in the flesh of human beings whom society judges as exiles or strangers to the norms of the times.

In our own era, the media have made us aware of the presence of "exiles" in our midst. Faith-filled individuals and socially responsible commentators have made us deeply aware of the horror of racism in our society. Social workers and politically sensitive leaders have riveted our attention upon the ways in which a youth-adoring society has dismissed our senior citizens for the sake of convenience or under the veneer of responsible economic cutbacks. Leaders in social justice have brought important insight to our need, in a male-centered world, to examine carefully and critically the right to equality of all our sisters who have been consistently and scandalously disenfranchised because of their gender.

We are reminded by church ministers, health-care professionals, and civic leaders that the differently abled and those who suffer from diseases like AIDS are not our enemies but truly are our sisters and brothers who need our complete respect and welcome at the table of human loving. Indeed, philosophers and theologians, social scientists, and simply good human beings have all called us to the task of a critical, penitential, yet hopeful examination of the myriad ways in which we have been inhuman to one another, especially to those we have forced to be exiles in our midst because they are different from our self-imposed ideas of what is normal.

The biblical injunction not to oppress the alien, the exile, is a powerful statement. Much as Francis of Assisi discovered Jesus hidden in the guise of a leper, those who are exiled or judged unclean in our midst have something to teach us about human nature and about the person of God who loves us. Prejudice and bigotry are not genetically coded into human experience. They are learned behaviors. They are born of human fear and anger. They are part of the ugly panorama of grave human sin. They can be countered and healed only with the remembrance of the God within each of us who knows that all of us in this world, in the final analysis, are truly exiles searching for a lasting home.

Our task is to loosen our angry, fearful, sinful fists and transform them into open, welcoming hands extended in love and unjudging care to those who have been oppressed or denied the equal, human, and social rights that belong to every person by nature of our being human.

Exiles in modern society are those of us who are lesbians, gays, and bisexual persons, known in some circles by the shorthand term "lesbigays." Lesbians, gays, and bisexual persons have always been present in the world. Though often without social visibility or equal human rights, we have been members of the human family in every epoch of history. Differing from culture to culture over time, our identity and life have been judged in various ways. In some cultures and in some ancient eras, we were respected members of tribe, state, and family.

In modern times, lesbigays have had the sad experience of being forced to live in "the closet," in virtual denial of the people that God made us to be. Like other exiles, we have known oppression and fear. Unlike other exiles, however, we have had to be truly invisible to others and often to ourselves. We have lived in terror of and in anger with those who have denied us our full and equal share at the human table, in the workplace, in housing, and in the simple joys of human freedom. Yet we are indeed everywhere, and many of us embrace our faith in Christ vividly and tenaciously precisely because we lovingly embrace our identity and life as lesbigay persons.

In the last thirty years, lesbigay individuals and communities have made significant inroads toward becoming full, visible members of our society, willing to struggle for the same inalienable rights as all other persons. This task has not been easy nor has it been completed.

Lesbians still experience a double oppression because of their gender as well as their sexual orientation. Bisexual persons sometimes suffer when gay or straight people refuse to accept that sexual orientation can be more dynamic than this-or-that categories. Gay men struggle daily to resist the world's damaging stereotypes, unworthy and false cartoon images that seek to rob them of their inherent dignity and fundamental identity as human beings. And for those of us in the lesbigay community who hold to Christian faith commitments and have withstood prejudice within our religious traditions, we have been challenged even within our own social circles as to why we would want to continue as members of churches in which we have not been made to feel loved, welcomed, and respected.

Despite continued deep and painful disagreement within modern Christian experience, many church communities, including the Roman Catholic and the Episcopalian, stand by the fundamental dignity of lesbigay persons precisely because we are made like every other human being: in the very image of almighty God. Some church communities have even taken the step of including antidiscrimination ordinances within church regulations or bodies of canon law.

Lesbigays have learned that we have gifts to share for the building up of our world and of the Reign of God. Like the disciples in the upper room, our journey from a fear-filled invisibility has been overtaken by the strong power of the Holy Spirit, who invites us to leave our fears and go out into the world and preach Christ in a new Pentecost of justice and peace for all the exiles of our world. As persons who love deeply the Christ who loved us first, we are committed like all other believers to the tasks of justice and peace. In the spirit of Pope John Paul II, who spoke in the same way to all believers, we have nothing to fear within ourselves. When our fears are melted in the fire of the Holy Spirit and redeemed by Christ, we can lay our gifts at the service of the world, at the service of our churches, and especially at the service of all those exiles for whom this world is still a vale of tears.

This volume of prayers and meditations is not an argument about the lifestyles that we live as lesbigays. Rather it seeks to link our faith-filled experiences with the biblical and historical tradition of "exiles" whom society has rejected, but in whom God's presence is as manifest as in any other human being.

This book is a gift from our lesbigay experience to all our sisters and brothers in the faith. Indeed, we are reminded in popular literature that "we are everywhere." This book is saying the same thing. We are here. We are in the world. We are lovers of God, too. We are your brothers and sisters in Christ who live and work in the world as companions in the human enterprise of heralding the justice and peace of God's Reign. With all people, we love God so much that our sleeves are rolled up for the loving labors of Christian prayer and Christian service: praying and working for the freedom of every human being to live in a world that can one day be at peace with itself.

Edward F. Gabriele
and Stephanie R. Gray

Preface

This book has been forty years in the making. Our forebears who spent forty years wandering in the desert after their Exodus and before their entry into the Promised Land provide a resonant image for my personal pilgrimage. For the Chosen People, the post-Exodus experience of the exile was a time filled with many contradictions and privileged memories. They were made to become radically dependent upon God for their daily food and safety. They had to confront strange peoples who endangered their security. They also had to face the idolatrous spirit of distrust within them that kept them tempted by the golden calf. It was the same for me.

Ever since I was very young, I knew that something was different about me. From early in life, I took an "exodus" from myself and wandered like an exile in many deserts. Despite the inevitable pain, it was a privileged time in retrospect. It compelled me to become deeply dependent upon the God of my understanding who nourished me when I could not nourish myself. Strange moments were mine. There were threats—many of them. I ran from golden calf to golden calf seeking the gift of self-worth in every place except where God had placed it, namely, within myself. Finally, after my forty-plus years of wandering, something new and fresh dawned inside me. I came to love myself in the way God had loved me, the God who made me as I am. No longer could I seek my meaning from all the lovely things outside me that had been mine. The God within me called me to a newer and unanticipated promised land.

Today I count myself as a gay man, a disciple of Jesus, a professional theologian, and an ordinary human being trying to be at peace with myself, with my God, and with my companions on this earthly pilgrimage. For all these things, I am grateful and delighted. In the spirit of gratitude, delight, and Christian service, this work came into existence.

This is not a book seeking to validate or defend members of the lesbian, gay, and bisexual communities, referred to in popular language and in this book as "lesbigays." The book simply seeks to link prayerfully the social exile of lesbigays at the hands of the world with the ancient and venerable metaphors of spiritual exile that are part of the heritage of the Judeo-Christian tradition.

Our spiritual tradition teaches us that every human being is the very presence of God. The Scriptures prophetically remind us that this is especially true of those who have been forced into exile or who have been made the victims of oppression and human bigotry. If we are to be true to our living tradition of faith in Christ, then we are called to honor those who have suffered and have been made to wander in the desert as outcasts. This volume embraces the experience of lesbigays as societal exiles and tries to illuminate that experience with the wider theological and spiritual base of our faith. God's grace burns especially in places where humans would prefer to ignore it.

Pope John Paul II is often quoted as saying that we have nothing to fear inside ourselves. Indeed, that could not be more true. Nonetheless, history reminds us how tragically we have been terrified of our differences from one another, often persecuting people for being different from ourselves. The long and shameful story of our inhumanity to one another has sometimes been written in blood.

Yet our Christian faith teaches that each of us is graced and blessed by virtue of our being part of the human community and the created order. Despite whatever misunderstandings and fears the world may have, our faith tradition compels us to proclaim that the presence of God is as richly and warmly alive in those of us who are members of the lesbigay community as it is in every other woman, man, and child.

When I first felt my "difference" some forty years ago, I never would have dreamed that I would write this book or claim my inner name, my gay identity, as a grace and a gift in a publication or any other public forum. This step, taken with some trepidation, is only possible now because of many others who helped me find the strength of Jesus Christ within me. Most of them must, for the sake of brevity, go unnamed. They are all held in my heart with great love and gratitude. However, there are a few that must be mentioned.

With particular affection I am grateful for the spiritual friendships of Barbara Tucker and Denise Douglas, whose personal ministries to me and whose warm affection shaped by their experiences in Christian marriage and motherhood helped me to come to accept and love myself. I am deeply grateful for the gifts of complete acceptance, care, challenge, laughter, tears, and love that I have known in fellow Christians such as my friends Joe and Ramona Lessen, whose warmth and love have been nothing short of the presence of Christ to me when others were less than welcoming.

I am indebted in gratitude especially to Stephanie Gray, close friend and lesbian sister, who coauthored this volume's foreword. Stephanie remains for me a constant, faith-filled, challenging, and patient companion, ever listening to my fears and angers, my dreams and hopes. I am further grateful for Brian Kline, whose strength of conviction helped me to critique my assumptions about my world and my faith in a new way once I had accepted myself.

Also, I am profoundly grateful to my close friends Stephen, Paul, and Richard, to whom this work is dedicated in a special manner. As each of the four of us came similarly to experience a harsh and unexpected price at the hands of others for claiming our previously hidden selves, our mutual and ever growing bond of charity and friendship helped to give shape to the syllables that found their way into this book. Finally and most importantly, I am deeply grateful for the support of Carl Koch and the staff of Saint Mary's Press who courageously supported, edited, shaped, and critiqued my work in this book. Without Carl's assistance, expertise, prayerful commitment to Jesus, and courageous witness to the cause of Christ's truth as the sole canon for all truly Christian publications, this volume would never have come to fruition.

It is my sincere hope that this volume of prayerful considerations can be a source of joy and abiding gratitude for all my lesbigay brothers and sisters for the many freedoms that increasingly are ours in these times. It is my further hope that this volume may be a springboard for a renewed sense of prayerful courage for those in our community who are still struggling in fear and the dark, deadly confines of "the closet."

Last, it is my hope that this volume can help all believing readers put to rest discrimination and come to appreciate that lesbigay Christians indeed are equally important and lively members of the Body of Christ, equal children of God, and inheritors of God's justice and peace entitled to the inalienable right of human dignity that Jesus won and crowned for every human being at cross and empty tomb.

"Something here broke the chains around his heart, and the voice from the bush kept saying: come closer" EX 3:1-4:17

Part A

Claiming Identity:
Marked with the Sign of Faith

Introduction to Part A

Claiming one's fundamental identity as a person is one of the most important tasks for every human being. Part of the very fabric of claiming our self is the ability to love our self precisely as God has made us. Claiming our identity and loving our self are part of the ongoing process of being continually born again as a human being, as a member of society, and finally as a disciple of Jesus. Being born is not something that happens only once when we leave the womb. Being born is a never-ending process that is the discovery and love of our self, of other human beings, of all creation, and of God. At times, this process of discovery is a joyful and exciting adventure. Equally, this process can be terrifying and the cause of great anxiety.

In the life of every Christian, part of the journey to claim our self in Christ is embracing ourselves precisely as God has made us. This ongoing experience is often like looking into a dark mirror. We do not know what we will see. As the medieval mystic Julian of Norwich pointed out, the pathway to God begins inside us. Coming to see Christ within us begins with seeing ourselves as human beings and loving ourselves honestly and with tender care. In coming to claim and love ourselves exactly as God made us, we come to a new sense of purpose, a new sense of freedom. We experience a new Exodus from all the pressures that attempt to make us be something other than the people God called us to be. In embracing our God-given identities as individuals, we shed the shackles of the self-hatred that robs us of our dignity, our liberty, our freedom to pursue all the ways God asks us to be the presence of Christ for one another. Certainly, there is a price for claiming and loving ourselves. We run the risk of rejection and of having to stand up for ourselves in a world that too often is fearful of differences.

Christian martyrs of every age have had to run ultimate risks. Jesus suffered the ultimate price. In the end,
however, running the risks of self-ownership and a healthy
self-love are unavoidable tasks in the quest for authentic and
lasting spiritual health and well-being. In the end, like Jesus,
running the risks leads us to the power of hope and the Resurrection. In the end, the price for denying ourselves and
thereby denying Christ within us is far greater and more
dangerous: our surrender to the terror of despair and self-
hatred.

For those of us who claim our lesbigay identity as a gift
from God, we may smile when asked why we would come out
of the closet when we know the price. Our smile is our witness to a new Exodus within us. We smile because this new
freedom today makes us wonder why we were ever daunted
in the first place. Our smile is a feeble reflection of the God
who smiled at us when first we looked honestly into the dark
mirror and saw Jesus within us. Daily now we look into the
mirror of ourselves, and we see and love the crucified and
risen Christ.

1
In the Beginning

Presence | Recall the loving presence of God.

Reflection | Whenever we wake from sleep and enter a new day, we face the mirror and see ourselves. Despite all the failings of our life, God has made each of us to be the unique individuals that we are. From the very beginnings of our spiritual heritage, we have been consistently reminded that God has made all of creation and that creation is good. Nothing that God has made is evil or destined for anything other than God's love.

However, numerous moments in life may tempt us to believe that there is something shameful in us. Certainly, we have failings. We sin. Sometimes events fall upon us that make us doubt our inherent creation in the image of God. Underneath our failings, though, is the consistent presence of God's goodness and love. For those of us who are lesbigay, each day calls us to the gift of courage: to believe in ourselves and in our inherent godliness. This can be part of our gift to the whole Christian community: the tenacious witness of a gifted and humble belief in self in a world that too often capitulates to the evils of bigotry and discrimination.

Canticle | **Genesis**

In the beginning
of every day and every night,
the Spirit of God hovers over me
and brings me into birth.
God speaks and light is cleaved from darkness.
God speaks and green things grow.
God speaks and the beasts roar and birds sing,
the clean waters gently brook through many fields,
and the day lily raises up its trumpeting orange
to blaze in greeting to a rising sun.

God speaks and the dusk gently falls.
God speaks and the silent, comfort-clicking of the crickets
lulls my world into a restful, grateful sleeping.
This is the garden into which God places me.
God has fashioned me with a tinker's hands.
In the image of God I am made,
and for God I am made to be a delight
to play before the God of all creation
and to proclaim God's goodness to every living thing.
Yet, there were many days when I was not so grateful.
There were many, many dark times
when the night-beast's roar was a demon's terror
and not a welcome song of strength proudly ruling the forest
     green.
There were many, many desert days
when I wandered lonely in a cloud of sadness,
an exile from myself,
angry at the moment of my creation,
believing that I was, in the end,
God's mistake.
But I was the one mistaken.
My mistaking was my misshaping.
I was no half-formed creature
made so by the judgment of hateful hands
or the apathy of those who simply would not look at me
really, truly, and in my flesh.
On a seventh day in an unnumbered year of my life,
God rested
and gently laughed with sheer delight.
God asked me to sit down beside a green pasture, a spring
     brook,
and gently rest and join the laughter.
Something poked at my ribs.
There, in my ribs, there had been a wound.
Something had been ripped out of me.
I had done the ripping.
God took that wound and gave it flesh again
and gave me to myself as my first companion
and taught me how to laugh.
On this seventh day in an unnumbered year of my living,
God and I rested from our labors,
God's grandeur of creation
and my sad attempt to rob it of its dignity.

There on that seventh day
God taught me to laugh once again,
and suddenly
I had a new beginning.

Reading | Jeremiah 1:4–10

Now God's word rang in my ears, and I heard God's voice say to me: "Before you were born, before you entered into the world, I had knit you together in your mother's womb. I made you. And I have loved you. You are mine. I poured oil upon your head and consecrated you for myself as my beloved messenger, a prophet to every people and nation." Hearing these words of delight, I trembled with disbelief and fear. Knowing myself and my innermost secrets, my soul was caught between these words of wonder and my doubts.

I responded to God, "Look at me. You know me for what I am. You know me for who I am. I am nothing. I am small in your sight and in the sight of the world. I am like a child to whom no one pays much mind."

Then God said to me, "Do not say to me that you are like an unnoticed child or that you are nothing in my sight. I have made you. I have fashioned you and that is your glory and your gift. I place my words in your mouth and my grace in your flesh. I appoint you to speak my word to every people and nation, to announce my year of favor to all you meet." Then God stretched out a loving hand and touched my lips tenderly. I left the presence of prayer and went out into the streets to announce God's favor to all who walked, like me, in fear and shame.

Intercessions | With joy we celebrate that God has fashioned us and all of creation to be the image of the Divine Presence in the world. Confident that our life can proclaim God's grace, we pray: Hear our prayers, O gracious God.
- For all the gifts of creation made manifest in the lives and works of every people and nation throughout the world, let us pray . . .
- For those who live in shame and fear, that the Holy Spirit may melt their hesitation and guide them to accept the goodness of God within their life, let us pray . . .

- For the members of the lesbigay community and for every person, that our life may be a courageous witness to the world that each and every human being is given their inner dignity and worth from the loving hands of God, let us pray . . .
- For all who work to raise up those who are bowed down, that their ministries may teach the world to lay aside the weapons of bigotry and discrimination, let us pray . . .
- And for our individual needs . . . , let us pray . . .

Closing

O God of Creation, from the beginning you fashioned all things to make manifest the wonders of your love. You do not scorn those that the world judges to be unlovely or lacking in worth. Rather you choose the world's exiles to speak your prophetic words of comfort and strength. Look upon all those whose lives are filled with shame and fear. Wipe away their tears. Raise them up. Remove the weaponry of hatred from your earth. Shape us all into the one family of your love filled with the spirit of the goodness of creation. We ask this, as all things, through Christ in the unity of the Holy Spirit, with you, one God, forever and ever. Amen.

The Lord's Prayer. Abba in heaven, your name is holy! Your justice come, your will be done, on earth as in the heavens. Fill us this day with all that we need. Teach us to heal as you have healed us. Bring us not to the test, but deliver us always from the power of evil. You alone are God, and all belongs to you!

2
The Word in Our Flesh

Presence | Recall the loving presence of God.

Reflection | Each year, Christians remember the birth of Jesus on Christmas Day. Our celebrations of Christmas often obscure the underlying and original message of this great feast. Sometimes this is the case even in the most sincere attempts at popular religious celebrations of Christmas.

From a seasoned reading of the Scriptures, the celebration of Christmas is about the surprising belief that in the birth of Christ, almighty God completely embraced our human nature. In the birth of Jesus, we celebrate and remember that there is nothing in human life that God has not loved and accepted into the Divine Nature, that there is nothing in creation that is not destined for the fullness of God's Reign. For many of us, this perspective on the Christmas message and thereby on the whole of Christian life is difficult. The judgments of the world can obscure our joy in our inherent goodness and God's choice of our very selves. Lesbian, gay, and bisexual believers and all believers who embrace their identity and their faith are living witnesses that God's grace and choice are irrevocable. Like children who are among the most vulnerable of human beings, lesbigay believers announce to all their Christian sisters and brothers the love of God that is the universal and authentic source of every person's inner dignity.

Canticle | ## An Escalator Christmas

Up a blustery escalator
at the end of a work-a-world day
to find oneself
rather in a window.
There in front a simple woman
carries a child
who himself carries
the window of all the world.

He smiles a wide-eyed smile
a Native smile
and seems to know all that he can know.
He reaches from his mother's arms
to grasp what looks delightful
the arm of a grown-up man
all wrapped in window-polyester
smelling like a work-a-world day
proud with pride's ambition
yet shrinking from the touch
of a simple Child
who knows only how to be delighted.
The Child's grasp;
the man's shrink;
the chase Eternal.
And this is what this Christmas-ing is
this forgotten remembrance
in a polyester world:
that the God who blusters above us all
comes to us in a Grasping Child
a Child whose Grasp is only for Delight
and yet we shrink and shiver
at the thought of such a Loving.

Luke 2:1–14

Reading

Now in those days, a message went out from the authorities
of the world that all people were to be counted as in a public
census. This message was sent to every province and city.
As good citizens of their world, Mary and Joseph went out
from their home to register in the place of Joseph's birth,
Bethlehem, the city of David. Joseph was of the house and
lineage of David. Now Mary was expecting her first child, the
child announced to her by the angel. So, Joseph and Mary set
out upon the long trip from Nazareth in Galilee to Bethlehem in Judea. What was a long trip for those times probably
seemed longer still for a man and an expectant woman. They
arrived. By tradition, their arriving may have been late at
night. They sought shelter. By tradition, there was none.
No one had any room for the poor. No one had another mod-
icum of space for these weary travelers; and it was close to
the time of her delivery. Somewhere they found a small
shelter, probably with rude barnyard animals. Her time
came. Among the common things of life, she gave birth
to her firstborn son. Among the common things of life,

she wrapped him in the fabric of their poverty. Among the common things of life, she laid him in a feeding trough, the animals probably quite annoyed that the presence of this tiny, pink, wriggling human baby had spoiled their evening snack. But he was born—the uncommon God delighted to be enfleshed in the common things of creation. The Son of the Most High come fully in the flesh, born quietly while the rest of the world was not listening. But there were shepherds listening to their sheep in the nighttime. A light encompassed them. Unbelieving, they thought they heard an uncommon message about an uncommon birth. The shepherds rejoiced and went to find a mother, a husband, and their child. An uncommon glory was gracing their land—grace upon grace was giving new meaning to the word *human*.

Intercessions

Caught up in wonder at the God who has chosen to pitch a tent among us and become one with our life, we pray:
Hear our prayers, O gracious God.

- For all Christians, that the message of Christ's birth in our midst may give us a new and abiding understanding of the dignity of each human being, let us pray . . .
- For our lesbigay sisters and brothers, that the incarnate Jesus may lead us through their example to appreciate the indiscriminate gift of God's choice in our life, let us pray . . .
- For all those who are denied the inner dignity of any human being, that the spirit of conversion may lead us to set aside the evils of discrimination and fear, let us pray . . .
- For all who live in fear and the shadow of death, that the power of the Holy Spirit may set us free, let us pray . . .
- And for our individual needs . . . , let us pray . . .

Closing

O God, in the birth of Jesus, you revealed to all the earth the fullness of your plan for our salvation. Born into our flesh, in Christ you embraced the nature of your children and granted us a vision of our worth and goodness. Do not permit us to sit in the shadows of fear and shame. Give us new courage to boldly accept your graces in our life. Teach us to love ourselves; and in loving ourselves, help us to teach all the world how we might love one another. We ask this, as all things, through Christ in the unity of the Holy Spirit, with you, one God, forever and ever. Amen.

The Lord's Prayer. Abba in heaven, your name is holy! Your justice come, your will be done, on earth as in the heavens. Fill us this day with all that we need. Teach us to heal as you have healed us. Bring us not to the test, but deliver us always from the power of evil. You alone are God, and all belongs to you!

3
Beyond All Fears

Presence | Recall the loving presence of God.

Reflection | One of the most difficult tasks for many of us is the achievement of self-esteem. Self-esteem and self-appreciation are important and inherent needs. In the evolution of our individual maturity, our understanding of our identity and our healthy self-acceptance undergo constant challenge. Yet without coming to some measure of self-esteem, a human being can sink into the mire of despair.

God has made each of us to be a unique presence of the God-Self. Our spiritual heritage has always held to the basic belief that the glory of God is the human being fully alive. Unfortunately, many of us have had experiences that have eroded our self-respect and healthy self-love. Lesbigay people, because of the sad history of human discrimination, have won the gifts of self-respect and self-esteem often at a great price. Some of us in the lesbigay community understandably hide out of fear. But we are called like every human being to leave behind our fears and embrace life and faith with courage and dignity. For those of us who embrace our lesbigay identity beyond all fears, even at the risk of misunderstanding or cruelty, the Christian community and the world receive a gifted witness of God-given courage.

Canticle | ## Papershade Prison

From behind the parlor window shade
she looked at the world
seeing folks go back and forth
to school and work
one with them
and then again, not one of them
never quite feeling that she belonged.

Jailed by memories
locked away from human conversation
a mocking memory kept her from the human touch
that lets the past be past
and makes past pain's power
dissolve into laughter.

Her middle-age eyes glazed by too much whiskey
narcotic before the power of this hidden pain
jealous of the workaday walking of other folks
whose lives seemed free and without care.

Hidden from their view, so she thought,
so worn she couldn't even wring her hands
just seated in apathy and pain
she could live without a life
and wonder all the same
if life was worth the living all the more
"If only they knew . . ."
"If only they knew . . ."

A secret. Always the same secret.
Some hidden life not meant to live in darkness
but see the light of day
and be planted in some garden where it could grow
and become what its seeds were meant to be.
But so many years ago
told that such a secret was worth a'shaming
she tucked it up
and hid herself behind this papershade prison wall.

Such is the way with closets and prisons
papier-mâché jails made with the hands of fear.
Neither is healthy for children or seeds
or anything that wants to grow.

And "if only they knew?"
Well, perhaps "they" might not care
and if they do
perhaps they might sing!

Reading | Genesis 3:1–15

In the early dusk when all the earth cooled, the Garden-Maker walked among the green things, searching for the man and the woman. The Garden-Maker looked under every leaf and blade. They were not to be found. Even in caves and beside the tall grasses by the River of Life, they were nowhere to be seen. The Maker could not hear their breathing. There was no sound of newborn human laughter and delight. It was as if the joy the Maker had given to the world was suddenly silent. It seemed as if the power of death had slithered into the garden unobserved. The Garden-Maker called out to them and heard them suddenly hold their breath into a gasp. That was the sound of something new, something not intended. It was the sound of fear. Slowly from out of a clump of tall grasses, they made their way before their Creator with eyes downcast and heads bowed. The woman and the man huddled closely to each other trembling. The Garden-Maker noticed something very different from the last time they met. They were wearing stitched leaves covering their bodies. Yes, something new was here. Something very unintended. It was the presence of a spirit never meant to lurk in the Garden. It was shame. The woman and the man slowly met their Maker's eyes. In the passing of eyesight to eyesight, the Creator knew what had happened. They slowly told everything, including their blame of each other and the serpent. They had not believed their Creator enough. They had not trusted. They had taken matters into their own hands and believed the hissing lies of the creature whose tinsel-promises caused their sorrows. It was done. Nothing could undo the damage except for one thing: a promise. Another promise, but one that could only be born into the distant future. And ever since this time, each woman and man and child have had to bear the fruit of distrust. Ever since this time, human beings have had to tend the inner garden to weed out the produce of fear and pray that the Garden-Maker's seeds of love might flower into a time when fear would be no more.

Intercessions | Into our life, fear dawns from a very early age. Yet our God does not leave us to the power of fear and death. In Christ, we are given a new hope beyond the price of our original mistrust. That we may have the spirit of courage, we pray: Hear our prayers, O gracious God.

- For all those who live in fear of themselves and stand at the mercy of the power of despair, let us pray . . .
- For the gift of the Spirit's courage, that we may each claim God's gifts in our life, let us pray . . .
- For each lesbigay, for all people, that the power of human hatred that so often robs us of our human dignity may come to an end, let us pray . . .
- For those who courageously help others come to an inner peace and hope about themselves, let us pray . . .
- And for our individual needs . . . , let us pray . . .

O God of all love, from the very beginning you graced each human being with divine dignity. Truly the fullness of our life is your glory and our privilege. In Christ you crowned all creation with a dignity that should never be forgotten. Breathe forth the power of your Holy Spirit and cast out from our midst the clouds of fear and despair. Raise us up with Christ to our true dignity as your daughters and sons. We ask this, as all things, through Christ in the unity of the Holy Spirit, with you, one God, forever and ever. Amen.

Closing

The Lord's Prayer. Abba in heaven, your name is holy! Your justice come, your will be done, on earth as in the heavens. Fill us this day with all that we need. Teach us to heal as you have healed us. Bring us not to the test, but deliver us always from the power of evil. You alone are God, and all belongs to you!

4
Voices of Revelation

Presence	Recall the loving presence of God.
Reflection	The Greek term *kairos,* meaning "time outside of time," refers to those moments of rich significance when our intuition meets our experience, and suddenly we are keenly aware of the most important moments of our life. Perhaps we encounter *kairos* when we meet our beloved, achieve a life's searching, or bid our farewell to a dying friend. Most importantly, the term *kairos* refers to those moments when suddenly we catch a glimpse of the meaning of our identity and our life.

Whatever the circumstances, every human being, at odd and unexpected times, experiences these "times outside of time" when all the earth stands still and an inner voice speaks to us in unexpected ways. In our spiritual tradition, this must have been the experience of Moses at the burning bush on Mount Sinai. Mary's encounter with the angel was another. Jesus had an untold number of these experiences. We do as well.

For lesbigays who hold to a rich faith in Christ, the moment when we accepted ourselves despite the price and the risk was an encounter with God's living grace within us. Our experience of hearing God's call to us in our identity is a prophetic challenge to all persons of faith. To hear God's call demands an attentive heart, an openness to life, and the courage to carry out God's will.

Canticle	**Holy Ground**

A jealous blaze against an autumn dusk,
fire fingers folded in prophetic prayer
around a lingering summer green.
Protecting Something
that no human winter of deception could ever conquer.

My eyes were riveted upon what seemed at first
a simple scene of changing seasons,
yet knowing that something here was very different
than the ordinary progress of summer into fall.
Something pulled at my soul with remembrance.
Something seemed so very familiar.
Somewhere from within my heart—
a story of a mountaintop revelation
a tale where hearts and dreams breathed on one another,
where shoes were tossed,
and names exchanged,
and something new was told about each other,
where something new was hoped about each other.
Something long hidden but always suspected.
Something feared before that time with no rhyme or reason
only that hearts would be forced to claim
the Truth—and embrace it with fire fingers folded sturdily
with all the blaze of prayer and prophecy
around a center of green life
that, once revealed,
no winter of human denial could ever lock away again
or force to live in shame and fear.
All this happened a very long time ago.
Then I did not know its meaning.
With a jealous blaze some Voice of Truth
blazed forth and showed me the way inside
to find the Truth and hear its name
and love It as it always loved me.
No more fingers of accusation with words of shock
        returning.
Just a simple smile. A calm accepting "yes"
to Freedom.
Without shame, without guilt
without any fear of fearful minds
or even angry fistful words.
Just a sense of wonder
for a name that God dared to give me,
for a life that now I would not trade
with all the things the world judges better.
For every time I see the autumn touch the world
like living things that blaze without being burned,
I think back upon those days and remember
that I have walked on Holy Ground.
And now, again I toss off my shoes with gratitude.

Reading | Exodus 3:1—4:17

Bleating sheep forced Moses' bleeding feet to climb the jagged rocks in search of possible strays. This day was no different than all the others since he fled his homeland after the unfortunate murder of that officer who was beating a slave. This hard life was quite different from the purple-cushioned comfort of those years of plenty. There were no springtime rituals beside the fertile Nile. Life now was a jagged affair peppered only with the wafting smells from hungry sheep. A simple life. Consistent and hidden. Comfortable. Up he climbed expecting nothing other than the daily routine of tending sheep against robbers and wolves. An ordinary life in land barren from riches and the complications of the court.

The sheep had beaten him to the top. No sign of marauders. His eyes caught a strange flickering glint. The sheep seemed to have grown strangely quiet. Perhaps his curiosity drowned out their usual bleatings for grass and water. Something seemed to reach inside his chest and grab his soul, pulling him forward to this thing that his mind simply would not accept. It looked like an ordinary bush. But the bush was encompassed by fire without its leaves being consumed. Like any other mortal, he wanted to run, but the faint memory of his responsibilities made him think of the sheep, and his earnings, and the anger of Jethro if he left his charges. He peered in curiosity and fear.

The unexpected happened and stole his breath. A voice called from the bush. He fell to the ground and his sandals seemed to fly from his feet. Something here was far from ordinary. Something here might be holy. Something here told him his life was about to end, that the ordinary humdrum of his daily bread would no longer fill his belly and his hidden, comfortable life. Something here was beckoning him back with a message of freedom and truth and justice. Something here broke the chains around his heart—a portent of stronger chains about to crack away from the ankles of his people back home. And the voice from the bush kept saying: "Come closer."

Intercessions | Into each of our lives, the invitations to grace come unexpectedly from the hands of a God who chooses carefully the moments when to be revealed. Knowing that our life is fed by the graces of God within us, we pray: Hear our prayers, O gracious God.

- For all Christians everywhere, that we may be open to the invitations of God in our life despite all costs, let us pray . . .
- For those who live in fear of the graces and gifts that God has given us in our identity and in our life, let us pray . . .
- For all the members of the lesbigay family of faith, that our acceptance of God's gifts in our life may be a source of courageous testimony to all believers, let us pray . . .
- For those who serve God's people in the ministry of counsel and direction, that their gifts and generosity may be a source of healing and courage to those whom they serve, let us pray . . .
- And for our individual needs . . . , let us pray . . .

Closing

O God of all graces, you called Moses at the burning bush on Sinai's height to be your instrument of freedom to those who were in slavery. In the fullness of time, you sent Jesus among us to seal that same message of freedom in the sacrifice of the Cross. Look upon each of us and give us the courage to accept your life within us and your call for our life's work. Give us new courage always to embrace your presence within us and to accomplish for you the works of freedom and truth. We ask this, as all things, through Christ in the unity of the Holy Spirit, with you, one God, forever and ever. Amen.

The Lord's Prayer. Abba in heaven, your name is holy! Your justice come, your will be done, on earth as in the heavens. Fill us this day with all that we need. Teach us to heal as you have healed us. Bring us not to the test, but deliver us always from the power of evil. You alone are God, and all belongs to you!

5
You Are My Beloved

Presence | Recall the loving presence of God.

Reflection | The waters of baptism free us from the power of sin and death, make us new creations in Christ Jesus, and seal us forever as disciples of Christ and servants of the world for justice and peace. Indeed, baptism is the primary sacrament of our salvation. In it we find a joyful and saving identity as human beings and as citizens of the world. The grace of baptism daily builds upon our human nature, and parallels our coming to embrace our fundamental identity as the unique persons that we are.

Traditional Christian spirituality looks upon the bath of baptism as a descent into the waters of chaos where Christ does battle for us with the ancient powers. Christ rescues us from the jaws of death and raises us up. In each person's life, there is a continual process of descending again and again into ourselves to discover fresh meanings. We are raised up to embrace our life and to contribute to the well-being and freedom of every person. As Christians we are taught that baptism is a "once for all" sacrament. However, baptism is really a "once for all" entrance into a process of self-discovery and re-creation of the self in Christ.

Lesbigay believers come to the waters of life with our fundamental identity and personhood. Each day, we enter again into the sometimes painful but essential process of self-discovery that is the task of every Christian, every human being. The tenacious commitment of lesbigay believers to our identity and to Christ Jesus is a fruitful witness to all Christians of our need to cooperate with the power of the Holy Spirit, who is ever deepening our life in the world and in Jesus.

Canticle | Carpe Diem

bare-knuckled grasping up against a blinding sky
fingers fixed forward

reaching to make a dream come real
black clouds and storm curtains
torn back before a clearing horizon
in the thin spaces between late lingering raindrops
a haphazard palette of fractured colors
splash across the newly cleansed air
like something almost dead
being slapped back to life by a fresh breeze
breathing in a swift, moist wind
my chest heaved
my arms grew stronger
reaching up
my bare-knuckled hands
upward and outward
reaching up with a frontier hope
to seize the bow
no more battles, the dying done
web-woven days and years of hiding now over
my death-denial pulled away from secret corners
the many-legged weaver of fear and despair
no longer laughs
but cringes in fear now that its power has been shattered
the weaver of nightmares is washed out
from the corners of my soul where he had nested for too
        long
no longer able to spin lies and half-truths in the night
my eyes are now newly open to the sunlight
I reach upward and outward beyond my self
to seize the bow
to grasp the hues of freedom
seize the bow and thereby seize the day
a New Day
and in that seizing and grasping
an echo of excitement bounces all around me
like the strains of music
which make the tiny dancer careen in joy
tempting me now to some different dance floor
to seize the music of a new song
to seize the bow of a newfound peace
to seize the colors of a rainbow of the soul
to seize a life without walls or inner prisons
to seize the Day
a Day of Going Forth
in Freedom

Reading | **Mark 1:9–11**

The muddy waters of the Jordan lapped at his legs just below the sand-encrusted ends of his camel-hair loincloth. To the general population, he was another of those curious itinerants who had long roamed the countryside, preaching loud and long about a coming savior. He was certainly more like themselves. He was far from the image of a rabbi or a Temple practitioner, much too rude a figure to be counted among the learned or the wealthy who had come to an arrangement with the Roman authorities. This John was a ragtag irritant to the powers at large. He did not fit their mold or their needs. He seemed to fit into another plan. Perhaps it was God's. Whatever the case might be, the crowds kept pouring into the region. Some of them accepted his water-bath. Perhaps they were happier now. Perhaps some hidden guilt was washed away along with the grime of field and marketplace. Strangely, some of the leadership had come too. They got much more than a water-bath in his words. One day it seemed that the earth held its breath when a man somewhat younger than this John approached the Baptizer and entered the waters. They had looked at and perhaps knew each other. There was some connection between them.

Without a word, the younger man unfolded his garments and knelt in the wading area. John with trembling hands scooped down into the river and poured the muddy water over the younger man's head and shoulders. It seemed like a moment caught in time. It all happened in the twinkling of an eye. Or was it a lifetime? Time seemed so stretched. They uttered no word between them. Only a long, deep glance as between kin, or between those who craft new ideas. No. Not new ideas. Something far deeper seemed to be passing between them. The younger man rose. He lifted his robes back around his olive shoulders. He looked up into the sky as if following a dove or hawk in flight. It seemed as if he looked a long, long time. He looked deeply serene, like one who has just been told that he or she is beloved. Maybe that is what passed between John and this unnamed man? Maybe the younger man heard some words of love? Maybe somewhere deep inside him he heard words that told him he was a beloved? Indeed, that would make a real difference to anyone.

Conscious that our baptism commits us to seize each day as a gift from God, we pray: Hear our prayers, O gracious God.

- For all Christians, that we may continually take delight in the gift of our vocation as baptized disciples of Jesus, let us pray . . .
- For all those who wrestle with doubts in their faith, let us pray . . .
- For the members of the lesbigay community, that the acceptance of their identity and their faith may be a witness of love to all people, let us pray . . .
- For all who shrink from accepting the daily graces that God extends to each of us as beloved children of the earth, let us pray . . .
- And for our individual needs . . . , let us pray . . .

O God, when John baptized Jesus in the Jordan, you plunged yourself into the fullness of our life. In Christ, you have given to the world the revelation of the full dignity of our human nature. Look upon all people this day and keep us mindful of our graced dignity in you. May we claim your love in our life. May we never deny to any human being what you have given to us all so freely. We ask this as all things through Christ in the unity of the Holy Spirit, with you, one God, forever and ever. Amen.

The Lord's Prayer. Abba in heaven, your name is holy! Your justice come, your will be done, on earth as in the heavens. Fill us this day with all that we need. Teach us to heal as you have healed us. Bring us not to the test, but deliver us always from the power of evil. You alone are God, and all belongs to you!

As if the World could not contain Her joy, she opened Her mouth and sang.

LK 1:26-56

Part B

Breaking Ties, Making Bonds:
Making the Choice for Christ

Introduction to Part B

From the moment that we enter this world, our life is marked by a never-ending personal and social formation to make all manner of choices for ourselves, for others, and for our world. Throughout the course of our life, every choice that we make has an impact.

Precisely because we are radically contingent and inter-dependent beings, our decisions make some deep and lasting impression upon us and those around us. Most often, the choices that we make are ordinary and imperceptible, like choices in personal preferences and interests. At other times, as in educational decisions or selections of career, our choices are more public and of greater moment.

Finally, into every person's life come those ultimate, almost irrevocable moments, like faith and love and political commitments, when we are faced with choices that can be definitive and monumental for ourselves and perhaps even for history. In the end, all of our choosings, whether awkward or smooth, entail the giving of a yes and at the same time a no to all the other possibilities that we might have made.

In the realm of our Christian faith, the hallmark of the Christian life has been the personal decision that individuals and groups make for Jesus Christ. In the earliest centuries of the church's existence, the choice for Christ was often marked by personal sacrifice, possibly even persecution and suffering. The milieu of Rome did not lend itself to an easy, comfortable way of choosing Jesus and renouncing all others. Often, families were torn apart, friendships and lives shattered.

After Constantine, Christianity eventually became wedded to the social fabric. Being a Christian was expected. Not to be in the fold was considered odd and a reason for becoming a social outcast. Generations of Christians were brought into the church without assuming the need for ongoing personal conversion into the person of Jesus.

The contemporary church urges us to understand that the quality of our Christian commitment is directly related to the daily development of a faith-filled yes for Christ. At the same time, contemporary believers appreciate that giving our no to those forces that do not reflect the life-giving presence of Christ can be an exacting demand.

For members of the lesbigay community, our decision to own our identity, our dignity, and self-worth was often a painful choice. Over the centuries, lesbigay persons have been forced to hide out of fear of persecution, rejection, and physical violence. For complex historical reasons, lesbigay persons have been stereotyped, shunned, and shamed into believing that we are unclean. Yet for many, gradually, a marvelous awakening has taken place within ourselves of the wonder, beauty, and dignity that God has given us precisely as we are as human beings—lesbian, gay, or bisexual.

Lesbigay Christians know the meaning and price of making a choice for a vision of the world where every human being can live in justice and peace, a choice for Jesus Christ who is truly present within us as Christ is present within every human person. For lesbigay believers, to say yes to Jesus is to say yes to ourselves and to all people. Christ bids us to be stewards and disciples.

At the same time, our yes to Christ impels us to speak our no to every force and power within us and without us that is not human, humane, responsible, loving, compassionate, strong, prophetic, and thereby Christlike. As we daily seek to love ourselves without fear as God has loved us first, as we seek to love the whole world as faithful disciples of Jesus, we stand like every other Christian beside the Cross of Christ, proclaiming with all our sisters and brothers that like Martin Luther: "Here we stand. We have no other choice."

1
Out into the Desert

Presence | Recall the loving presence of God.

Reflection | In the story of Christian spirituality, many individuals made a choice for Jesus Christ that cost them dearly. In fact, embracing Christ always has some price. Each time that we give our yes to something in life, we say no to countless other possibilities. This is part of humanity.

Whether it be the choice of a life partner, a school or career, or the purchase of a home, our choices call us to die to all the other alternatives. We do not have the ability to calculate the full cost of our human choices or of our choice for Christ. For some believers, choosing Christ literally cost them their life. For most of us, choosing Jesus costs us old values, comfortable attitudes and behaviors, friends, and sometimes family members who disapprove of our commitment.

For lesbigays, the stark yes to our identity necessitates that we leave the oppression of the closet. This may cost us friendships and family ties. Many of us have lost jobs. Some of us have known blatantly hateful words or actions against us. Sometimes leaving the closet makes us outcasts. For believers, choosing to embrace our identity is an explicit act of choosing the Jesus within us. This applies equally to lesbigay believers, and we know the cost. The testimony of our choosing, despite the price, is a witness for all Christians of the courage it takes for anyone to choose Jesus.

Canticle | ## Scapegoat

wild-eyed with terror at the sand before his feet
the rage of a nation laid lately on his head
echoes of derision still sounding in his ears
with hands trembling at unknown prospects.
behind him lay years and years of history
the memories of promised and everlasting affections
of eternal loyalties
of those who had called themselves so glibly "friend."

no more.
stripped of every mask
stripped again of every dignity
laid upon the wood like an animal in sacrifice
accusing sneers had pierced hands and feet.
but nothing, nothing could compare
with the razored lance of abandonment
which had torn his heart in two.
ripped from every familiarity
and told he was "unclean"
he knew the unknown before him
was far and away the better choice
than what had gone before.
he did not need to shake the dust from his feet
his footsteps were no longer welcome
at the doors of those who lately
had gone from friendship to something other.
yet the weary undoubted lifelong task
of tending bitter memories
could never, ever dilute the sweet exhilaration
of freedom's blessing born of cursings.
inside him something stirred.
now that the fever had been broken
and the unlulled pain from piercing dulled,
another memory, a deeper mystery
another once had gone this way
and stood beside him presently.
suddenly a whisper out of nowhere
spoke of choices
knit from the moment of the womb
not of simple human preferences or evanescent whims.
claiming riches unable to be claimed by time
or changing habits of the fickle human heart
or shallow acts of human politics
or transitory canons born in fear.
a choice for freedom
choosing riches that are within.
he chose.
one feeble, trembling foot
stepped out upon the desert sands.
and then, what had seemed so filled with terror
was only warm, familiar, inviting.
home.

Reading | **Genesis 21:8–20**

Here we are. Driven out into the desert. I was the wife of Abraham. I bore him this man-child, this Ishmael. He was Abraham's firstborn when it seemed no other would be the fruit of his loins. My Ishmael came filled with promise. But when Sarah gave to Abraham the man-child Isaac, the eyes of jealousy were opened. Perhaps she feared that her Isaac would never know the affection of his father. Such is the way with firstborns. They inherit everything these days. The price of such jealousy is this desert trek we have before us. Only a small portion of water and bread is ours, and it soon will be consumed. We have been driven out into the wild with the beasts. Because we were looked upon as a threat, now we work our way in a desert surrounded by threats. Jealousy has given way to the brutality of rejection. And we walk in fear. Mine it is to protect this child of my womb. I would give my life for him for he is mine. Perhaps I should bow down and die so that he may live. But what is this I hear. Something like a distant voice is speaking to me. Something tells me to look. There is a water well for our refreshment. Perhaps all is not lost. Perhaps the God of Abraham did not make us for nothing. Perhaps God is with this child, and he shall grow strong to give praise to the God who saves the desert exiles.

Intercessions | God has called all believers to honor the presence of the Almighty in those who are most downtrodden. That we may sense the presence of God in every exile we pray: Turn to us, O loving God.

- For all those who are impoverished by human hatred and discrimination, that God may teach us to honor their humanity in Christian welcome, let us pray . . .
- For those in our midst who, as prophets, call our attention to the needs of human dignity, that we must give to poor and exiled people, let us pray . . .
- For people of the lesbigay community who have been made exiles by human ignorance and fear, that the example of their courage and faith may be the beginning of God's freedom for all poor people, let us pray . . .
- For all those whose hearts and words are the source of human oppression, that the power of the Holy Spirit would move them to lay aside the weaponry of hatred and bigotry, let us pray . . .
- And for our individual needs . . . , let us pray . . .

O God, in the poor and the exile, you have told us that you are most abundantly present. When you came in the person of Jesus, you walked among us as one of the lowly. Open our eyes. Rid us of the narrow vision that is ours. Drive human hatred from our midst so that we will never again drive out the exiles and the poor. We ask this as all things through Christ in the unity of the Holy Spirit, with you, one God, forever and ever. Amen.

The Lord's Prayer. Abba in heaven, your name is holy! Your justice come, your will be done, on earth as in the heavens. Fill us this day with all that we need. Teach us to heal as you have healed us. Bring us not to the test, but deliver us always from the power of evil. You alone are God, and all belongs to you!

Closing

2
These Bones Shall Live

Presence | Recall the loving presence of God.

Reflection | Sometimes our decisions uproot us from our surroundings: from associates, friends, family, or life directions. Sometimes only mild changes greet our decisions. In other instances, our choices for life herald tragic losses. In times of great change, some individuals seem to lose everything around them and fill with inner turmoil, fear, and despair.

In the Gospels, Jesus fully appreciates the way the world would reject his disciples. At the cross, Jesus himself is portrayed as having lost everything in the way the world calculates such things. For lesbigay believers, to choose to leave the closet and embrace one's identity carries with it the full possibility of meeting uncalculated losses that can rob one's sense of self. However, for all Christians, there is the virtue of hope: not a naive belief that everything will turn out smoothly, but rather the strength to endure the challenges of the present. For all who choose Christ, the trials of the present are a premier opportunity to witness to a courageous hope that endures everything for the sake of the truth inside that is a mirror of God's loving will.

Canticle | **Dry Bones**

With a clatter like dry bones knocking together,
the phone receiver shook in its cradle.
Something bruised my intuition and I knew
that somewhere this was to be a hard conversation.
I never know why that happens.
But it is always true.
Somewhere, somehow my spirit alerts me
to these moments of choice,
these premonitions that something truly difficult but worthy
is about to dawn into my waking day.

I answered, picking up the clattering receiver,
only to be greeted by an icy voice that used to be familiar
in another time and another place
before all my questions had come to light.
Though sheltered half-safely in the same family,
the years had seen us drift apart.
I, immersed in questions unarticulated,
could never understand within me why I wandered.
Only that I sought some place of my own
free from a fear of suffocation and of being made into a mold.
She, driven by some need for closeness I could not give,
had made her angers and resentments very clear
again and again in letters and icy conversations
always crusted with indignation and a kind of wolfen-longing
that frankly was a source of terror for me.
As always, the conversation never included any questions
as to how my life progressed.
We only talked, as always, about the need for money
and how I, in my life, was not a partner for her perceived
        pains;
how I, though living at a distance, "should be" such and such
for her and for a mother trapped by their own choices and
        misdirections.
The conversation was like a well-rehearsed script
that never deviated from its substance or its style.
It seemed like some mad addictive cycle
that began the same, coursed the same, and never hoped to
        end.
It would come to rest this day as it always had
only to rise from its grave some other time.
Or so I thought.
For there, in the course of syllables of dollars and cents,
I made clear that life might deal me an unfair card
and I had to be prepared.
At which her rage poured out:
"That's because you're playing with fire.
You chose this life;
and now you'll have to suffer.
Let's cut it where it is and stay just merely friends
and nothing more."
I held my breath.
I felt caught as I had for all the years we played as children.

My stomach churned as it had those years before
when in her rage and sadness over anything
she would scream when our parents were gone.
And then, from out of nowhere, new words exploded
    in my gut:
"You're right. Perhaps that's all we are.
And nothing more."
Those momentary syllables were like a two-edged sword
that made their way across heavy chains laid on me for years.
I had claimed myself and my life.
I had embraced the inner name God gave me.
Suddenly I knew what had led me wandering from family
all those years before:
their unarticulated sadness and resentment,
their clawing at me and pawing at me
trying to deny who I am,
trying to force me to be something I cannot, would not be.
For I can never be a daytime
for their nightly, ghostly wishes.
I had, then, before me this utter, bare-boned choice:
to be myself and live
or live their lives and die.
I hung up the phone and knew a falsehood had come to its
    end.
The fever had broken. Sweat poured down my face.
I felt suddenly alone with a tempting liberation in my
    mouth.
I closed my eyes.
And I was whisked away to a field.
There before me I saw a vision of white bones strewn about.
A Voice told me to sing, and I sang.
The dry bones knit together.
Muscles covered those bones
and the air was filled again with Life.
No longer was there any clatter of deathlike conversations.
Suddenly, I was tall and bold and filled with life.
Knowing that another Hand
was knitting me all over again.

Reading | Ezekiel 37:1–14

One day I had a rare moment at work to catch my breath. I
closed my eyes and suddenly I felt as if I had been whisked
away from my place to stand in a field that was cluttered

by dry, dead bones. The vision struck me as rather curious. Lately, my life had been filled with the rupture of every connection that I had with others. Choices about myself had to be made. I had chosen, and opposition seemed to meet me on every side. I had lost family, friends, and career. Yet something in me kept hanging on despite the fears, the resentments, the angers, and the inner empty sadness that seemed to eat at me. And here I was. Standing in a field that bore too much familiarity to the map of my inner life. Dead, dry bones. Nothing more. An arid wind blew boredom. Even the smell of death and decay had gone. This truly was a place of nothingness, a place where life simply was over. Something moved me to walk among the bones. Something like a prophesy was spoken, and the wind around me picked up. A faint scent of springtime took the air. Springtime in this void? Impossible. And yet I could not deny the difference that was getting stronger in the air. I heard a clatter. Dead, dry bones seemed to be moving. They were being knit together. The wind strongly stirred the dust up. In the play of wind and sand and sunlight, muscles were being drawn on the bones. And flesh. And eyes and movement. And when the wind and sand died down, the dry bones had been replaced by an army of the living. Then the sun broke through like a smile breaking over the field. And in this smiling, incredible moment I heard five words inside me: "Hope, and you will live."

Though we meet difficult challenges in our life, God plants inside us the hope and strength to endure the present moment until the dawning of a new day for each of us. Confident that we are never left alone even in the darkest hours, we pray: Turn to us, O loving God.

Intercessions

- For all those who follow Jesus even at the cost of losing everything, let us pray . . .
- For those who seem to have great losses and are most tempted to despair, let us pray . . .
- For the members of the lesbigay faith communities, that their courage in being faithful to themselves and to God endures, let us pray . . .
- For all those who resist the hard decisions of the Christian life out of fear and timidity, let us pray . . .
- And for our individual needs . . . , let us pray . . .

Closing O God of every gift, into each of our lives you choose carefully your moments to invite us to grow more deeply as your children. When Jesus walked among us, you set before him the cup of your divine will. Breath your spirit of life into us that we may gladly embrace your will even if the cost is great. Give us the spirit of hope when we suffer for the sake of your justice, your peace, your compassion, and your will. We ask this, as all things, through Christ in the unity of the Holy Spirit, with you, one God, forever and ever. Amen.

The Lord's Prayer. Abba in heaven, your name is holy! Your justice come, your will be done, on earth as in the heavens. Fill us this day with all that we need. Teach us to heal as you have healed us. Bring us not to the test, but deliver us always from the power of evil. You alone are God, and all belongs to you!

3
A Song of New Life

Presence

Recall the loving presence of God.

Reflection

Though differing by degree, our choices give way to unexpected situations that take us by surprise. Many times, choices filled with fear and ambiguity become a prelude to new and exciting moments, totally unprecedented or unanticipated. The bleak moments give way to bright times of renewed freedom and joy.

Such was the case for the early disciples of Jesus who hid fearfully in the upper room. The Holy Spirit brought them out into the daylight in strength and freedom to preach the Good News. Indeed, the freedom that comes after giving our yes to Christ and to our life can make us wonder why we were ever fearful.

For lesbigay believers, the moment we decided to accept our identity—a moment we feared would bring us rejection—gives way to a new sense of inner peace and freedom that is a gift of God. God does not will for us to hate ourselves. God desires us to love ourselves and celebrate ourselves in the same measure that God loves and celebrates our creation. Though we mature and develop afraid of the world's judgment, lesbigay believers who come to know the freedom of Christ inside ourselves have an opportunity to witness boldly and joyfully to Christ in our acceptance of the inner name of our life. To do so is to leave fear behind and to open our arms and life to joy, to raise our voice with a new song that can bring hope to everyone hungry and thirsty for God's mercy and freedom.

Magnificat

Canticle

With the cold clatter of an iron gauntlet
thrown down before a combatant,
the letter fell from the postal box
with the dull thud of challenge.

He had waited ages for this news
and perhaps had guessed its contents all along.
How much he would have given
to have his voice sing Freedom once again.
Years ago, by lying and ill lips accused,
his voice had been silenced,
his singing had been stilled.
Years later, by written and repentant words,
his name had been rebaptized
if for no others, at least for himself.
He had sought once again
to have his voice sing out, his heart be free,
his feet lead his friends in the dancing.
He came before the council of his world
and asked them once again to let him sing.
They thought and pondered.
They questioned and consulted.
In the end and only for the cause of politics and fear,
they wiped clean their hands.
And pronounced him, "risk,"
too inconvenient
for the Word which never knew convenience.
The leaden letter lay heavy in his hand,
its polite politics heavier in his heart.
There for them was no proven innocence
without some suspected prior guilt.
The guilt had not been in the lies.
The guilt was judged
because he claimed his loving name in freedom.
The origination of this original distrust
was not in him but in his elders.
With irony they passed its burden down to him.
They connected so sinfully his hidden name
with lies that had no life or substance.
The marriage of past lies and present fear
seemed to be the collusion that would render him silent.
But could it?
Could the marriage of politics and convenient distrust
silence him forever?
Like Balaam needing to listen to his ass
he needed to look to another pathway.
For God does not know only one road
for the service of the brokenhearted
and those whose lives are more deeply marred

by the shadow of death
and the cruelty of despair.
Suddenly and without warning:
Sadness gave way to anger
and bitter resentments melted
before the birth of something new.
The lowly are not condemned to be down-trodden.
The down-trodden have the way to the heights.
The hunger within him saw another Banquet.
Yes, suddenly without warning,
without human reason
or that logic that makes us think
that every defeat is final,
he burst forth in a new song to the God
who was calling him to yet another Path.

Luke 1:26–56

Reading

Not long before, this very young woman in an ordinary life
had met an uncommon stranger who told her disturbing
news that had stretched her soul to its limits. By our standards, her place in her social climate was alarming. As woman and as seeming child, she was not even counted in the
population. Her world always made her gender to be the
property of men. She was not even permitted to sit at the
feet of teachers and learn the life of the Law. Her lot was to
be married, to bear children, to be obedient and silent in the
synagogue and Temple. Her world would never let her move
in freedom among the tents of her people. But an extraordinary visitor had brought her news that she dared not speak
in public. He placed before her the consummate question:
Would she do God's will, absurdly as it sounded? She had
wrestled with the visitor's question. She wrestled in what
must have seemed more an eternity than a second. Inside
her, her childlike love of God made her know that what she
was asked to do was indeed right and good. Yet there was the
price. The price: to conceive a child, holy or otherwise, outside the confines of her society's marriage laws. Unthink-
able. Laughable. A reason for being stoned and killed. Even
so, something inside her made her say yes. She did not know
why. She just spoke the word. And the Word became flesh.
And when she spoke, her world cracked open before the
Word. Her life and the life of the world would never, ever be
the same. Afterward, knowing there was a need, she made
haste to help her kinswoman, an elder who was with child

but much outside her expected time. Mary picked herself up. It seemed as if her yes made her feet move more swiftly to the needs of her relative. Her bowing to the will of God made the ears of her soul more attentive to the cries of the poor. She made haste to be of service. And there, greeted with words of praise she never thought would ever be said of her, she could not contain her joy. Slowly but finally, it dawned on her that her soul was not tapping in time with a music ever heard before, but only dreamed within her. And as if the world could not contain her joy, she opened her mouth and sang.

Intercessions　With our surrender to the will of God in our life, there comes upon us an unspeakable joy and an inner peace. In thanks for the loving will of God in our life, we pray: Turn to us, O loving God.

- For all Christians everywhere, that we may be made bold to hear the word of God and put it into practice, let us pray . . .
- For those who wrestle with the movements of the Spirit in their life, that the Spirit of courage may be their consolation and their strength, let us pray . . .
- For all who struggle to come to inner peace with the inner name that God has given them, that the Creator may wipe away their fears and strengthen them to embrace the divine will gladly, let us pray . . .
- For all members of the lesbigay community, that our witness of self-acceptance and service may be a gift to all believers, let us pray . . .
- And for our individual needs . . . , let us pray . . .

Closing　O God of all life, you called Mary to surrender to your will and thereby become the mother of the Incarnate Word. As Mary gave birth to your Word, first in her heart and then from her womb, so may your Holy Spirit move your faithful people to embrace your Word in our life and then place it into practice by a life of service. We ask this, as all things, through Christ in the unity of the Holy Spirit, with you, one God, forever and ever. Amen.

　　The Lord's Prayer.　Abba in heaven, your name is holy! Your justice come, your will be done, on earth as in the heavens. Fill us this day with all that we need. Teach us to heal as you have healed us. Bring us not to the test, but deliver us always from the power of evil. You alone are God, and all belongs to you!

4
Simple Gift

Recall the loving presence of God.

Indeed, we sin. Indeed, we fail. Yet the authentic message of
the Gospel declares that human nature at its roots is blessed
by the Creator. In this spirit, the rich and enduring spiritual
heritage of our faith reminds us that acceptance of God's will
entails a commitment to lay our gifts at the service of God
and others. As our life opens and changes over the years, it is
our responsibility to respond to God in new ways. What we
have been given by God can enrich others and make our
world a better place.

    Sometimes the hardships of our life or the choices we
must make open unexpected doors for service. For lesbigays,
the experience of rejection or the experience of new associates and circles of friends can be exciting invitations to lay
open our gifts for the glory of God and the betterment of
others. The Creator invites each believer to search out the
Christ in other people and then to serve in ways she or he
can. This service of others gives full credence and visibility
to the Word. Thus, the world is enriched, and her or his
example becomes a leaven of love and service among all
people.

Gold, Frankincense, and Myrrh

Red-cheeked with piercing eyes offset against the cellar gray
that danced with me from the deepest human listening
to an infectious laugh which seemed to make
    the wood shake,
he sat behind his desk all during the last hour
chain-smoking and sipping greater cups of coffee.
Not so many weeks ago, I had made an unexpected departure
from my former way of life.
A newer Voice within me had called me to
    yet another journey.

I had no idea where it would lead me
except that it would happen step by step.
I was caught in that moment in-between
the breaking and the bonding
wondering where by and by
the invitations of another season might lead me.
Hopefully, they would lead me to some measure of peace.
No job, little money, a temporary arrangement for the
    moment.
That's all I had at this juncture.
And then I had read an ad,
a chance to put my hands to another plow.
That ad had brought me to this moment,
with this thinning man whose infectious laugh
seemed to fill the room and shake the rafters,
this monklike man whose deepset listening
seemed to fill me in a strange new way and shook my fear.
This was a momentary moment
on a pilgrimage of grace,
the end result whenever one's Yes to Life
becomes the moment to say No to what has been.
Perhaps like others who had made this same journey,
my mind had soaked in its share of confusion,
and I needed a place to wring out all the liquid memories
that crashed upon me every night, wave upon wave.
He invited.
I spoke.
I told the story of my journey thus far:
how my newfound freedom had cost me so dearly
and had brought me to this moment where I had nothing
but was free.
He held his chin in one hand as he leaned back
rocking on his desk chair.
He made that kind of lowing syllable that makes you know
that something important just might come next.
Like an ancient wise companion
he helped to put together the pieces of my life's puzzle
for the moment
and told me that the future was not his to predict.
However, he could assure me just as surely as he was there
that this in-between moment of my life was another
    discovering,
it was my finding of the gift within me

so that one day, somewhere, somehow
I could offer to my God
a gift I never knew I had to give.
Suddenly I closed my eyes and felt a winter breath across
    my face.
It seemed that my knocking at his door this morning
was my knocking at a stable long ago.
Other companions, truly more wise than I,
had already come and laid before a shivering Child
their coffers of gold, their frankincense and myrrh.
The Child looked at me and made a newborn smile
or so I thought.
And I knew that this time more than ever
I was asked for my gift,
my gold, my frankincense, my myrrh,
my life
such as it is
just as it is
and nothing more.

Acts 4:32—5:11   Reading

The early followers of Christ were gathered in a communion
of hearts. Indeed, they were one mind, one heart, one life,
and one love in Jesus. Nothing that they did was for themselves. Each gave all that they had for the service of one
another. No one ever went hungry. No one ever went thirsty.
No sorrow was mourned in solitude, but each bore one another's burdens. No joy was celebrated without giving forth
the goodness of Christ to all the sisters and brothers. Indeed,
all that they had was held in common. No one's needs were a
burden. Every gift was shared and built up the whole community of believers. There was no one needy among them.
Indeed, their giving itself was like a sermon of great power
and witness to the presence of the Risen One in their midst.
And God added greatly to their numbers. Yes, they loved one
another. Some even sold homes and goods so as to feed the
poor and the lowly. But into their midst one husband and
wife held back some of their proceeds. Their selfishness was
like a death. They held back and did not give. And so the
whole community was seized with fear: fear of what a selfish
heart can do; fear of what a selfish heart can deny to the
least in the world.

Intercessions | God has graced each human being with dignity and gifts that can feed those who hunger for compassion and strength. In thanks for all that we have been given and interceding for the strength to be generous, we pray: Turn to us, O loving God.

- For all Christians, that our life may be marked by the generosity of Jesus especially to those who are most in need, let us pray . . .
- For those who are caught in the power of selfishness, that the Spirit of God may move them to a greater love of others, let us pray . . .
- For all who suffer from a spirit of confusion and are in need of the Spirit's direction for their life, let us pray . . .
- For the witness of lesbigay believers who accept God's invitation to new and abundant pathways of generous service for others and the world, let us pray . . .
- And for our individual needs . . . , let us pray . . .

Closing | O God, from the dawn of creation you have graced us with your dignity and called us to love one another deeply and without reservation. In Christ, you walked among us and touched our life, filling us as you always do with all that we need. Look upon your faithful people. Teach us to give to others as you have given to us. We ask this, as all things, through Christ in the unity of the Holy Spirit, with you, one God, forever and ever. Amen.

The Lord's Prayer. Abba in heaven, your name is holy! Your justice come, your will be done, on earth as in the heavens. Fill us this day with all that we need. Teach us to heal as you have healed us. Bring us not to the test, but deliver us always from the power of evil. You alone are God, and all belongs to you!

5
A Life of Blessing

Recall the loving presence of God.

To give one's life over to Christ is to make a conscious choice to reject the powers of evil in oneself and in the world and to accept the life of God. To accept God's life is to embrace a new way of living that is a daily deepening in love, mercy, and a passion for God's will alone.

To choose God's life can be a source of tension and conflict. Jesus suffered the ultimate price by giving his life out of love. When we follow Jesus in accepting God's presence as our life, we enter into a lifestyle most eloquently articulated in the Beatitudes. The Beatitudes have been called the Magna Carta of the Christian life. Not a legal blueprint in the ordinary sense of law, they capture poetically the hallmarks of authentic Christian witness: being peacemakers, merciful, willing to suffer for the sake of goodness, centered only on God's will. For lesbigay believers, to claim our identity is to make a deliberate choice for the blessings that God has planted within us despite the misunderstandings and unfortunate discrimination we have experienced in society. As Christians, we are called to be people whose life is marked by the blessings of the Beatitudes. Our effort to live out the Beatitudes is a unique blessing, challenge, and witness for all believers.

Beatitude

across the lane from milling crowds
gathered on a dimly green lawn
waiting to hear some word of human wisdom
waiting to be touched by something
to make them larger than themselves
hungry for a human touch
thirsty for anything that might make sense of darkness
    and despair

the poor in spirit gathered in a place of homeless poverty
bound by some primal urge to run from fear itself
leaves had curled in the wind
joining in the flight from fear
tree limbs stripped of their summer best
were twisted in the wind like human arms
reaching upward and outward
reaching anywhere from the earth's confusion
like a lost child looking for a set of stronger arms
to take away the terror of the nighttime
a small crowd of tattered people
with tattered souls from a shredder world
a small crowd that had at first stood apart from each other
circled slowly closer to one another
drawn in by words of warmth
spoken in the middle of sharper winds
ever closer ever hoping
for a word of comfort
a word of meaning
hungry ears in which still echoed the death rattle of
    thousands
thirsty hearts in which the pang of human suffering
made dull the other human needs of bodies
we stood
hoping to catch in his syllables
any glimmer of hope against which the night could be
    conquered
like a hillside long ago
this ragtag group of pilgrims
had given everything
had left everything
had renounced every other hunger
for a Word of Life
cracked lips parted and wet cheeks formed words
praying here in the late-year autumn
praying with a deeper dignity
integrity marking every prayerful song
eyes peered into a simple human loaf of bread
heartsick loneliness and hungering despair
were lost in a ceramic-pooled cup of wine
lost amidst the elements
but not forgotten
only sung into significance
and prayed into a deeper dreaming

joined hand in hand by newer bonds of charity
crumb and sip joined together in eternal time
nourishing eternal hope
words ancient ever new
words to calm the fears
to soothe the angers
to rouse lost hopes
"blessed are the poor in spirit—
theirs, the Reign of God."

Matthew 5:1–14 Reading

The Teacher saw the multitude and something stirred within
him. They looked so hungry, so thirsty. Something in him
knew that their hunger and thirst were not really for bread
and water. Something in their souls begged to be fed. Perhaps it was that inner emptiness that was always there. The
rule of Rome over them had only hollowed out their emptiness more and more. The empty words of many of their religious officials made the emptiness even deeper. He could
sense those soul-words that cried out, "When, O God?" He
climbed the rocks to what seemed like a mountaintop. He
opened his mouth, and his simple words seemed to quiet the
agitation of souls and limbs. "How blessed are you poor,
God's Reign is yours. Blessed those who weep, they shall
have comfort. Fortunate are the humble, theirs is the soil of
life. Happy those who hunger and thirst for what is right,
they shall have their fill. Fortunate are those who give mercy, for they shall have it in abundance. Blessed are those
whose eyes are fixed on God, they shall always see their God.
Blessed are those who work for peace, they shall be called
God's special children. Blessed are those who suffer persecution for the sake of truth, theirs is God's Reign. How blessed
are you every time you are persecuted or suffer your names
and life to be broken because of me, you shall in the end be
rewarded. Be of good cheer for you are in good company. The
holiest of prophets were treated in the same way by the
world. Indeed, each of you is salt and light. Each of you is a
blessing for all the world. If you hide your gifts or lose your
flavor, then it is only poverty that is born. But when you give
forth your light and the gifts of love within you, then all the
world is filled with the goodness of God. Let others see your
good gifts and thereby give glory to God!"

Intercessions From the mountaintop, God has called us in Christ to be a blessing for one another and for all the world. Strengthened to live the Beatitudes each in our own way, we pray: Turn to us, O loving God.

- For all Christians, that the Beatitudes may be the hallmark of our every work and love in the world, let us pray . . .
- For those who suffer because of their witness to Christ Jesus, that God may strengthen them in their trials and give them courage, let us pray . . .
- For lesbigay disciples of Jesus, that God may lead us to new ways to live the life of grace and thereby enrich the whole church's acceptance of God's will, let us pray . . .
- For those who are caught in the dark forces of evil and resist the power of Christ's love by their fear and lack of charity toward others, let us pray . . .
- And for our individual needs . . . , let us pray . . .

Closing O God, at the dawn of creation you made us as women and men of love. You fashioned us in your own image and crowned our life by the presence of Jesus among us. Give us the courage of your Spirit to look deep within ourselves, accepting and loving ourselves as you love us. May our acceptance of ourselves be joined to our acceptance of your will in our life. Make our life a blessing for others and for all the world. We ask this, as all things, through Christ in the unity of the Holy Spirit, with you, one God, forever and ever. Amen.

The Lord's Prayer. Abba in heaven, your name is holy! Your justice come, your will be done, on earth as in the heavens. Fill us this day with all that we need. Teach us to heal as you have healed us. Bring us not to the test, but deliver us always from the power of evil. You alone are God, and all belongs to you!

god touched
me, gentle
as the
breeze
upon
my shoulder

I KINGS 19:11-18

Part C

Finding One's Place:
Discerning the Invitations of Grace

Introduction to Part C

None of us is born into a vacuum. Our birth makes us heir to many legacies. We are born into a specific family, culture, community, nation, religious background, language, social and economic stratum, and lifestyle. We enter human life as members of many groupings. These are the grounds of our being. We can remain in these groupings for life. We can choose to leave them. In the end, life still invites us to find our place daily and to "make something" of ourselves.

Our task is to engage in the surprising, sometimes very frightening, process of discovering how we fit into the various communities. We discover how to creatively use our human inheritances and make some measure of contribution to ourselves and to our world. The discovery of ourselves, our world, our talents, our potentials, and our limits is both frightening and ecstatic. It is part of our search for our place, our need to see where and how we can belong.

The history of Christian spirituality gives lively witness to the need for believers to discern our individual place as women and men of faith. We are called to discern the spirits and signs of our life and our times. As baptized persons, our first commitment is to Jesus present in the course of our daily living. God's will for us is manifested exactly within the movements and opportunities of our days and nights.

As theologians have always reminded us, grace builds upon nature. God does not call us to be anything or anyone other than the persons God shaped in love and tender purpose. The grace of God builds upon our nature, our unique personality, our innate or developed human gifts, and the real limits that are simply part of our being human. There is no single, normal way to be human. There is no single or best way of being Christian. Our task is to discern the ways in which God is calling us to give unique witness to God's Reign.

Like all Christians, lesbian, gay, and bisexual people attempt to see how we can fit with one another, fit into our world, fit into God's plan for creation, and thereby offer our gifts to a very hungry world. This requires discernment of God's graced invitations in our life.

1
Everywhere

Presence | Recall the loving presence of God.

Reflection | The Second Vatican Council made an important statement in the *Pastoral Constitution on the Church in the Modern World*. The participants crystallized in that conciliar document what has always been true of Christians: we are citizens of the world with a message of hope to every age, every nation, and every person. Whether as prophetic leaders of the church, as concerned legislators whose values of goodness and compassion influence public policy, or as ordinary members of a nation's workforce, Christians are called to make a positive difference in people's lives. All of human life can be touched for the good by our service as disciples of Jesus.

The same is true for lesbigay believers. In every place, we are called to make a positive and productive difference. Our faith and our identity are a fertile source of witness and service to the church and to the world. With all Christians of every time and place, lesbigay believers can rightly say, "We are here. We are everywhere. And with you we can make a difference for Christ and the world."

Canticle | **Present Always**

subway doors parted
she walked into the crowd
amid laughing youth
and tired middle age
slowly plodding her way
past laughter and fatigue
to find a seat
the wrinkles of her face
stood in stark contrast
to the days-end polish of the weary
and the afterschool delight of the young

it was the end of their day
but just another hour of her own
with shopping bag
and pink-scarved head
and overcoat with collar wrinkled upward
she resolutely made her way to a seat
with deep black eyes
to match her mother's skin
and gray wisps poking drolly
from beneath that weary scarf
she stared into the crowd
knowing them but not knowing
standing off and standing near
making a statement like of old
i am here to stay
no harsh word no arrogant stare
just that strange sort of looking
that lets you know someone is there
with a secret
that escapes the weary
and gets drowned out by the laughter
but remains all the same
and simply says
someday you will know
someday you will know

2 Corinthians 4:7–15 | Reading

In us, we have a vast treasure in clay vessels. The treasure
is not ours. It is God's. It belongs to God alone, but we are
stewards of it. All the power we have within us comes from
God, flows out from us, and is meant to give glory to God
alone. We have known hardship for this treasure within us.
We have been persecuted in every way for our discipleship in
Jesus. We have been afflicted, but not crushed. We have been
confused and perplexed, but never driven to total despair. We
have been the object of persecution and lies, but we know
that we are not forsaken. Some of us have been struck down
by violent hands, but we have not been destroyed or removed
from the face of the earth. We are always carrying in our
bodies the death of Christ until he comes again. In carrying
the death of Christ within us, he is made visible through us
to all the world. For while we are alive, we are given up to

the powers of death and destruction for Jesus' sake, so that Jesus may be made visible in our flesh to every creature under heaven. We are confident that the promises of Christ are ours. Indeed, with Christ, we shall be raised up from the violence of this world. We are called to take our place in this world with all disciples so that the grace and salvation of God may be extended through our witness to every people, to every time, to every human heart that longs for peace. And in all this, we give thanks.

Intercessions

God has formed us as a faithful people in Christ to bring the good news of salvation to the ends of the earth. That we may rely for our strength upon the power of the Holy Spirit, we pray: God of exiles, hear our prayer.

- For all believers, that we may be faithful to our witness of Jesus Christ despite all costs, let us pray . . .
- For those who are searching to know God's will for their service of the world, let us pray . . .
- For all the members of the lesbigay community, that our life may increase the witness of the churches to God's compassion and peace, let us pray . . .
- For all who refuse to hear God's truth in the message of Jesus, that the Holy Spirit might open their heart and mind, let us pray . . .
- And for our individual needs . . . , let us pray . . .

Closing

O God, you are the source of every good gift and the author of all life. In Christ, you have called us to be a faithful people, bearing your truth to the ends of the earth. Look upon us and give us your strength that our flesh may be a living witness to your compassion. Do not abandon us when we suffer, but make us joyful in the knowledge that our presence in the world can give glory to your name. We ask this, as all things, through Christ in the unity of the Holy Spirit, with you, one God, forever and ever. Amen.

The Lord's Prayer. Abba in heaven, your name is holy! Your justice come, your will be done, on earth as in the heavens. Fill us this day with all that we need. Teach us to heal as you have healed us. Bring us not to the test, but deliver us always from the power of evil. You alone are God, and all belongs to you!

2
Wondering

Recall the loving presence of God. Presence

Conversion rarely occurs automatically. The act of religious   Reflection
conversion, like human birth, is never neutral. Whether
gently or in strength, conversion is always an entry into a
process that inevitably reshapes and refashions one's entire
life. Conversion normally happens in the midst of questioning and confusion. During the time of searching, an individual attempts to understand what it means to be converted
into the person of Jesus. Necessary questions arise: What is
really being asked of me? What will my future be like? How
is my present life being changed? Do I have the personal
courage and conviction to survive these changes? All of these
questions, and many more besides, become the focus of one's
heart and soul.

    Understandably, these questions can propel us into a
time of intense ambiguity and fear. However, the grace of
conversion is such that God stands very close to us when we
attempt to discover our place and how we have been called
deeply into the person of Jesus. For lesbigay believers, the
act of coming out of the closet is normally followed by a
period of exhilaration and confusion, a sense of freedom but
also questioning. How will I survive in the world? What is
God asking me to be and to do now that I have embraced my
identity? Every Christian must face these questions in the
light of one's ongoing conversion into Jesus. The wrestling
and questioning, the confusion and wondering are all a dramatic witness to the simple reality that conversion into Jesus
is never truly simple. It makes demands and calls for intense
personal reflection until that time when the Holy Spirit
makes clear to us how we are being asked to live and work
for the Reign of God.

Canticle | *Ad Saecula Saeculorum*

Like an aging star still twinkling
he looked over the edge of a cheap, glass tumbler
the glint of his eyes
mixing with scotch and soda
and the sparkling lights around him
engaged in glasslike conversation.
He dove into a pool of memories
of days and years before his temples grayed,
before his belly filled out
before his dreams bottomed—
memories of longing
of hoping for some kind of loving
that could make the circle of his empty arms
less a burdened fear.
Around him the music wafted in and out
lyrics with no apparent meaning
a beat with no apparent ending.
The music-wisps of conversation,
the kind that signal the end of another day of work,
bounced off glass and ears.
The latest sale, another movie,
the latest move of an unfriendly politician,
another gathering, talk of a new love,
broken dreams and broken promises laughed off nervously
as if this is the way it always has to be
ad saecula saeculorum. . . .
Glasslike glinting conversation
bouncing from beat and lyric
adding to the dulled but persistent shine of his eyes
further dulled by hopes unflowered and dreams forgotten.
One strand of his graying hair fell from his thinning
         forehead
right across his eyes and seemed to dangle teasingly into
         his glass
in which his eyes were riveted,
seemingly oblivious to it all.
But was he?
Did he seem not to hear and yet heard more loudly
than all the other patrons?
Did he seem not to care and yet cared more deeply
than all the others whose glasses, like his,
seemed to twinkle like so many holiday lights
against the dark shadowed closet of a room?

He grunted slightly beneath his breath
a kind of sighing sound that most would never hear,
a kind of grunting that most would always fear.
His uneasy movements on his seat from side to side
betrayed an inner ambling
perhaps an inner wondering
if he could escape from what seemed an eternity
of twinkling into a scotch and soda glass.
Too often life passes us by because we let it.
Because we do not seize the moment
love's possibility gets liquid-lost
words of caring are drowned out
by the relentless beat of empty lyrics
and all that seems left
is the sad odor of liquor-stained tumblers.
And then I realize, like another Dorian Gray,
I may be looking in a mirror.

Galatians 1:11–24 Reading

At one time, dear friends, I was chief among those who hated
the church of God. At one time, I laid violent hands on those
who followed Jesus. So content was I in my ways, that I
could not conceive of any other path. And I sought to elimi-
nate anyone who thought differently. One day, it seemed as if
something inside me cracked open. No one else did this to
me. Today I believe that it was the hand of Christ that
opened my mind and heart. Suddenly, I felt as if everything
around me was new and frighteningly different. I had no idea
what had happened. Today, I count it as the act of Jesus within me. Then, I was not so sure. I was confused and lost as if
blinded by something. I could no longer live in the world of
my past comforts. What was I to do? I had no other choice. I
had to leave the world of my companions and spend time in
the desert of my soul, pondering what all this meant. There
was a new path before me, and I feared it. No longer was I
the master of my life. Some unseen hand was weaving a
different tapestry inside me. I was led into the desert of my
questions, and there I wandered for what seemed to be years.
I could not go back to my former life. And I feared what others would think of me. Very slowly my questions gave way to
an inner conviction to embrace God's will come what may.
And so I did. Christ was now alive within me. I left my solitude and my questions and sought God's holy people. And
they gave thanks to God for what was being done in me.

Intercessions | In each period of our life, God calls us always more deeply into the life of grace. That we may be faithful to God's will despite our fears, we pray: God of exiles, hear our prayer.

- For all Christians, that we may boldly embrace the questions and invitations that God gives to us to deepen our faith, let us pray . . .
- For those, including ourselves, who fear the invitation of God to the spirit of continuing conversion of life into Christ, let us pray . . .
- For the members of the lesbigay communities of faith, that our witness to the struggle toward self-acceptance and working for God's Reign may be a witness of courage to all Christians, let us pray . . .
- For all those who are bound in a spirit of confusion and fear, that the Spirit may break through the clouds of their despair, let us pray . . .
- And for our individual needs . . . , let us pray . . .

Closing | O God, you designed us to be drawn into your embrace. You know our fears and our hesitations. When you call us, our heart grows faint at the bold designs of grace. Yet you do not leave us to our fears. In Christ, you always strengthen us. Breathe forth your Holy Spirit upon us. Strengthen us always that we know your will and accomplish it. We ask this, as all things, through Christ in the unity of the Holy Spirit, with you, one God, forever and ever. Amen.

The Lord's Prayer. Abba in heaven, your name is holy! Your justice come, your will be done, on earth as in the heavens. Fill us this day with all that we need. Teach us to heal as you have healed us. Bring us not to the test, but deliver us always from the power of evil. You alone are God, and all belongs to you!

3
Patience

Recall the loving presence of God.

The process of discovering God's will in our life definitely demands patience and reflection. More often than not, the will
of God is revealed to us gradually and often in the quiet
times. For hurried human beings, waiting on God's will can
be an arduous and painful task. We are not much used to
waiting.

Discernment of God's will demands an inner attentive-
ness to the signs of the times. Above all else, if we are to
discover where God is asking us to serve, we must be willing
to acquire the time-honored virtue of patience. A curious
word, *patience* comes from the Latin *patior* meaning "to
suffer with," implying to suffer with the present moment
until all things are made clear. Disciples of Jesus practice
patience when we put God's will into action before our own.
We practice patience when we sift through our ordinary
experiences and the grind of our daily living to discern where
Christ is asking us to foster justice and peace.

Lesbigay believers need to practice the virtue of patience to understand where we belong in our own community, in what new ways we belong in our family, in what ways
we belong in our world, and in what ways God is asking us to
serve our neighbor. By virtue of baptism, all Christians have
a priestly vocation. Indeed, we all have been baptized into the
priesthood of Christ to make the world holy. To discern how
we are to do this demands that we listen carefully for the
quiet presence of God who will call us to serve the whole
world in ways that may catch us and others by surprise.

Canticle | Dance of Desperation

Multicolored lights flew through festive air
and made the gathered dancers dance more swiftly.
Like children on a carousel
around the mind's eye they flew
as those who wished they could
watched on from leathered seats.
My head slowly turned
to review the scene passing by
to catch a glimpse of dancers and watchers
and the interplay between their souls.
From out the corner of my eye
I spied one man standing all alone.
There, with glass and cubes swaying and brimming,
he stared.
He reeled a bit from the contents of his glass.
He looked glazed.
But behind the glaze there was a wondering.
No one paid him much mind.
Little would anyone guess
how much he was paying in return.
Behind his eyeful glaze
there seemed to be a longing
something which betrayed a wishing
that he could make his feet spring free
from the clay of his desperation
and set them to the beat
of swirling lights and faced-past clothing.
Like one caught in quicksand
he seemed unable to be caught up
in the swift air around him.
He seemed to sink more deeply
into an eternal question:
"Is this where I belong?"
The laughter and delight
of dancers and watchers
was of no consequence to him.
Sealed off inside his question
he swayed with each new drop he drank.
No one invited him.
Perhaps that is what he expected.
But his shackles kept him earthbound
and uninvited by his own choosing.

Suddenly it struck me
I was looking in a mirror.
New to the happy dance myself
I knew that he was but an image
of my own eternal question:
"Where do I belong?"

1 Kings 19:11–18

Reading

Lately I had to flee from the rage of the royals. My life, my
words, my very presence had enraged them. Simply being
visible in their world seemed to drive them mad. I fled from
them in fear. Perhaps I did not trust my God very much. God
had made me a prophet. I was the messenger of God's word.
For it, I was made to suffer the rejection and rage of many.
I fled from the angry crowds. Perhaps I was fleeing from God
also. I ran away and hid in a cave on Horeb. So much I wanted the consoling presence of my God. It is not easy to be
called, to speak with the Word, to suffer for its truth. I entered the cave on Horeb and, praying with all my might,
waited for God to come to me. Sleep overtook me. Suddenly
and without warning the ground beneath me shook. Rocks
split, and I felt tossed from corner to corner of my refuge.
Perhaps God was in the earthquake. But God did not appear.
I fell asleep again and seemed to rest for just an instant. With
a crash that made my eyes open wide and my hair to stand
on end, lightning flashed around the cave. A storm had broken, and it seemed that the turmoil in the skies would swal-
low up the earth. The wind swept up everything around me.
I was afraid. Perhaps God would come in the power of the
storm. But God did not. Then, as suddenly as the storm had
broken, it ceased. A gentle breeze and a supremely different
sense of quiet circled around me. And then I knew. God
was approaching. And so I fell on my face and adored. God
touched me, gentle as the breeze upon my shoulder. And God
told me to get up and go back. Go back and open my mouth
in new ways. God sent me back to be a prophet: to announce
true royalty and a final freedom of the spirit. God filled my
legs with strength, and I went back to the world where I
belonged to preach the Word that possessed my life.

God calls each human being in ways mysterious that our
gifts and talents might be at the service of God and our
neighbor. Asking for the grace of discernment, we pray:
God of exiles, hear our prayer.

Intercessions

- For all Christians, that we may be open to the promptings of the Holy Spirit who enlightens our understanding of the path God is setting before us, let us pray . . .
- For those who are filled with a spirit of confusion, that Wisdom may give them knowledge and patience until the will of God is made manifest, let us pray . . .
- For all lesbigay believers, that the spirit of patience may strengthen us as God reveals to us how we might serve our neighbors and our world, let us pray . . .
- For those who fear what God may be asking of them, that they may know the comfort and patience of the Holy Spirit, let us pray . . .
- And for our individual needs . . . , let us pray . . .

Closing   O God of every good gift, you call each of us to serve you and the needs of the whole world. Limited as we are, you ask that we wait upon your Word to know our path in life. Open our mind and heart. Give us the gift of true patience that we may discern aright how we might bring the Risen Christ to others. We ask this, as all things, through Christ in the unity of the Holy Spirit, with you, one God, forever and ever. Amen.

The Lord's Prayer. Abba in heaven, your name is holy! Your justice come, your will be done, on earth as in the heavens. Fill us this day with all that we need. Teach us to heal as you have healed us. Bring us not to the test, but deliver us always from the power of evil. You alone are God, and all belongs to you!

4
Discernment

Recall the loving presence of God.

Ignatius of Loyola highlighted the necessity of discernment as the tool by which we come to discover God's will in our life. Discernment of God's will demands that we pray for the gift of wisdom, one of the gifts of the Holy Spirit. Far deeper than even the most profound human knowledge, wisdom was pictured by our ancestors in the faith as the woman who stood at the right hand of God. Christians ask for the presence of wisdom to sustain us in life and to help us know and follow God's will.

We need the gift of wisdom if we are to come to a clear understanding of the invitations of grace in our life. For lesbigay believers, living in a world that can trigger our resentments and fears, asking for the grace of wisdom is extremely important if we are not to retreat into ourselves or make our faith only a personal consolation. Each day, believers must ask for the gift of wisdom so that we may come to know God's will for us and to make God's will our primary task in life. We ask for wisdom to inspire us as we view all the choices that are laid before us. We ask for holy wisdom that we might make the best choices we can for God and for the betterment of the world. We ask for wisdom that we might turn from selfishness and embrace a way of living that is Christlike and generous.

Procession

Against the autumn chill and a swirl of fallen leaves,
I took a cold seat at the city's circle.
It was an ordinary day like any other,
a day I had away from my desk,
a day to amble through the city streets
and watch with curious delight the many on their busy way.

Of course, they did not know that I was watching,
and probably would not care even if they knew.
They merely had their life to live, their works to labor,
their many places the paths to which they took so quickly.
With the hurried steps of workers, indigents took an equal
    pace
hoping that some harried worker would drop a dime or
    dollar
just to rid them of the unwelcome company.
Pigeons and squirrels kept even time with the fast
    morning walkers
looking for a dropped crumb or kernel.
It was an ordinary day filled with ordinary people.
And then there was me.
Lately come to inner questions,
I wondered where I fit into the scheme of things.
Workers, wanderers, pigeons, and squirrels:
they all had their place in the city's circle.
I felt somewhat out of pace with their endless procession,
somewhat misclothed and out of touch.
I tried to blend my questions into the background.
But my questions would not let me be so blended.
I had questions to answer and wonderings to be confronted.
In my newfound freedom I realized only too well
where I no longer belonged.
For I was somehow different at this point
of the circle and procession of my own life.
A new rubric had overtaken my newfound resolve of self.
But every form of freedom needs its roots and ground.
And it was for them, root and fertile ground,
for which I was searching.
Do I be like the young and proud?
Do I emulate the older couple in their wisdom?
Do I look the part of the wanderer and stay lost forever?
Or do I be like pigeons and squirrels
looking to feed from someone else's dreams?
For, oh, so many years I never believed I could belong
to anyone or anything.
God knows, I tried.
And in my trying always failed.
Always there was the new group, the instant infatuation.
Always there were the inevitable misgivings
and the tarnish of reality
that led to harsh and often leavings.

Now, thinking I may have another chance,
I came here to see where I might belong.
And there were no answers.
For the answer now is the same as it always was,
the answer I had never let myself hear.
Where I belong is deep within myself.
Where I belong is in all the circles of the world.
Where I belong is with all the workers and wanderers,
with all the creatures that look for crumbs of loving
hoping against hope that someday, one day, anywhere
we might be everywhere together:
not aimlessly processing to madcap commitments
that have no lasting meaning in the end.
Rather for us to belong with and in one another
processing toward another day for every season
where crisp winds and human hearts
make us to walk with one another.

Wisdom 9:1–12

Reading

O God of all my ancestors and God of every freedom, you
have made all things by your word, and you sustain us by the
power of your spirit wisdom. By wisdom you formed us from
the clay and gave us breath. You have called each of us to be
steward of your world and your works. You have asked us to
tend the garden of your delights with tenderness, righteousness, and mercy. This day and forever I ask for none of your
gifts except that of Wisdom herself. Do not reject me as your
servant though I am poor and needy. I am your servant, frail
as I am in the eyes of the world. I am short-lived and weak. I
am simply a human like all others. Of myself, I have little
understanding of the world as it passes before me. Even if I
were to be perfect in every way that the world judges, I will
be nothing at all if I am not blessed by your gift of Wisdom.
You have chosen me to do your will, though often I am filled
with confusion as to the steps I must take on your pathways.
You have commanded me to build up the glory of your name
through all my world and to make of all hearts high moun-
tains of praise for you. With you alone is Wisdom. With you
alone is perfection. With you alone can all righteousness be
known and loved and lived. She it was that danced through
the world and brought your creation to life. She knows what
is pleasing to you and what is the right path for my life.
Breathe forth and send her to my side this day and always
that I may know and love your will and place it into practice.

Send Wisdom to lead me all the days of my life. Let her guard my every path and sustain my every work. Then shall I know peace and pass my days in your love.

Intercessions

To know the will of God, the gift of the spirit's wisdom is given to us. That God might open our heart to receive the presence of wisdom, we pray: God of exiles, hear our prayer.

- For all Christians, that we might pray each day for the presence of wisdom in our life, let us pray . . .
- For those who struggle to know the will of God and live it, let us pray . . .
- For lesbigay believers, that we may earnestly seek to know how God is asking us to serve the needs of the world in justice and peace, let us pray . . .
- For those who would deny to others their service of God and neighbor because of the sadness of human ignorance and bigotry, let us pray . . .
- And for our individual needs . . . , let us pray . . .

Closing

O God, in the beginning wisdom brought all creation to life. Indeed, wisdom enlightens our ways and helps us to know your will. Open the hearts of all believers. Help us to see your presence in our midst. Make quick our heart and hands to know your holy will and to put it into practice. We ask this, as all things, through Christ in the unity of the Holy Spirit, with you, one God, forever and ever. Amen.

The Lord's Prayer. Abba in heaven, your name is holy! Your justice come, your will be done, on earth as in the heavens. Fill us this day with all that we need. Teach us to heal as you have healed us. Bring us not to the test, but deliver us always from the power of evil. You alone are God, and all belongs to you!

5
Invited to Table

Recall the loving presence of God.

Presence

The invitation to the family table signifies a deep and abiding friendship and intimacy. In fact, cultural anthropologists and students of human ritual tell us that of all the many rites celebrated by human beings, the rituals that most frequently celebrate human intimacy are those of the table and feasting. To share food and drink is to share one's life. No wonder then that the stories of our faith often depict God's invitations to us as an invitation to a meal. All our life we search to find those tables where God is calling us to share the food and drink of love and the fullness of life.

Reflection

Jesus did not hesitate to sit at table with friends and especially with those whom society judged as outcasts. He invited all people to belong as full members of God's community. The eucharistic meal should still be one place where all people, without distinction and without discrimination, are invited as full and equal members. In many ways, discernment of our place in God's design is the discovery of the various tables to which God is calling us. The great sadness of human life is our refusal to feast with God and to feed one another.

Lesbigay believers, like all others, pass before many tables in this life. At some, God calls out to us and invites us to eat. At others, God invites us to wait the table. Our task is to discover where God is making which of the invitations. Our further task is to pray for the strength to accept God's call and to seize our invitation to belong to God, to each other, and to a hungry world in search of our loving service.

Pride

Canticle

Deadly sin or lively virtue?
The never-ending debate about human pride.
Without it we are told we cannot live,
but with it we are told we risk all other human vices.

83

Like a trapeze artist carefully balancing each step
to forego a drop into a dark abyss below,
so each movement of my soul progresses daily
between the pride that tempts me to believe I am a god
and the gnawing despair that makes me think I have no
    pride at all.
Caught between this awful juxtaposition,
this moment of life between Babel and hell,
I took a Sunday ride downtown
and found myself in the middle of a parade.
All manner of women and men decked out in rainbow
    variances
marching together, lockstep, arm in arm,
bursting at the seams with celebrations of themselves.
I wondered:
Is this our downfall? Is this our collusion with the fallen
    angels?
Or is this our claiming of an inner gift
still yet unappreciated by so many others?
There are those that think we rainbow people
have no pride, only despair.
There are those that think we rainbow people
are a sorry mark upon the world.
There are those that wish we rainbow people
would vanish from their eyes like a shameful memory.
I looked and smiled at the parade marchers,
knowing I was one of them and never could be otherwise.
I am part of the myriad colors of life that was marching by
in utter celebration of inner graces now appearing.
An Epiphany of Pride!
A bursting, swirling, dancing, singing Pride!
No Babel, no despair.
No cowering at the glum and dismal judgment of human
    fear.
No capitulation to the brute forces of worldly ignorance and
    rage.
No victory this day for those who would turn this dancing
    joy
from lively virtue into deadly vice.
I wondered.
Why would the world want to turn such pure, unfettered joy
into something dank and foreboding,
something to be hidden?

Why ever would the world wish to silence children in their
    laughter
and end the spirit that sets our feet to dancing?
Even from my sideline view,
my feet stepped in time with the music.
Though I did not know the name of any person standing
    near me,
I knew each one all the same.
And in knowing them the seams of my jacket burst,
my lungs filled with the festive air,
my fingers tapped the music's beat against my crossed arms,
and I became the music, the beat, the song, and the dance.
I was caught up in a rainbow of delights,
unfurled, full-bodied, unashamed,
and completely overtaken by real, earthy pride.
Yes, this pride is truly a risk.
It carries one outside all the restricting prisons and closets
that make a prisoner of the human heart.
This pride is no deadly sin.
It fills with life and so is worth the risk.
I looked again at the proud parade,
a long line of witnesses whose robes were washed
in the blood of an Ancient Innocent who calls us all to
    freedom.
The marchers carried palms of a newer century.
Their chants were to a different cadence.
But these proud witnesses were but the latest members
of the long line of martyrs who always have proclaimed
that death itself has died and Life Itself is immortal.
I looked at the proud parade of my sisters and brothers,
and I smiled.
Then I knew and dared to shout
from my soul's rooftop to all the world:
"I belong."

Luke 19:1–10   Reading

I was a little man, very short. More important than my physical size, my being short was the way I felt in front of others.
I never learned a trade. So, I became a tax collector. Not the
most popular of professions, but it was a living. Though I
could take a little share of the profits if I placed a slight pres-
sure of the thumb on the measuring scales, there was always

something uneasy in me when I did that and had to look into the eyes of a poor mother and her child. I never could find peace in myself in those days. The whispered resentments from passersby made me feel smaller than I was. And then there were the festivals when no one invited me to their table. One day, I heard that this wandering rabbi from Nazareth was passing by. People said he was a miracle worker. We had many such miracle workers in those days. But some people said he was different. He never collected money, never passed a plate for donations. He spoke with a gentle but definite authority. And he was kind. He never refused to eat with anyone, even those the priests said were unclean or damned. He was supposed to have been a generous man and made sure that no one around him ever went hungry. An extraordinary type of rabbi for our times. An unusual character. I wanted to see him very much. Perhaps it was just my curiosity that had the better of me. If nothing else, his marching by would at least relieve some of the boredom of my day. I always passed my days quite ordinarily, even taking my meals alone. So, I decided to see this rabbi. Being so short, I climbed a nearby sycamore. It looked strong enough to bear my weight. He passed by. He looked as ordinary as I am. And then suddenly he stopped, turned around, and looked straight into my eyes. He asked himself to dinner. I was dumbfounded. He invited himself to eat with me. A tax collector! I was so stunned that I felt like I wanted to give back all those slight shavings I had taken from the poor. Something told me that if I said yes, everything—absolutely everything—in my life would be different. And it was.

Intercessions

God calls us to be seated at table and partake of the food and drink of love and dignity. That we may be made bold to accept God's invitation and feed one another as well, we pray: God of exiles, hear our prayer.

- For all Christians, that our life in Christ may be an endless sharing of our love with those who hunger and thirst for justice and peace, let us pray . . .
- For those who are mired in unworthiness and refuse God's invitation out of despair, that God may lure them out of their fears and give them the courage to be fed in love, let us pray . . .
- For all who are searching for those tables where God is calling them to be fed and to serve, let us pray . . .

- For lesbigay believers everywhere, that we may be open to God's invitations in our life and celebrate our belonging as full members of God's family and the human community, let us pray . . .
- And for our individual needs . . . , let us pray . . .

Closing

O God, you are the source of dignity and the giver of every good gift. You feed us with our daily bread and with the cup of salvation. Send forth your Spirit into our midst that we may know the tables to which you are calling us. Give us the courage to let you feed us. Give us the strength to feed one another as Jesus has fed us all. We ask this, as all things, through Christ in the unity of the Holy Spirit, with you, one God, forever and ever. Amen.

The Lord's Prayer. Abba in heaven, your name is holy! Your justice come, your will be done, on earth as in the heavens. Fill us this day with all that we need. Teach us to heal as you have healed us. Bring us not to the test, but deliver us always from the power of evil. You alone are God, and all belongs to you!

"Bowing his head he breathed forth his Legacy" John 19:25-30

Part D

Suffering at the Hands of Fear:
Willing to Endure the Cross

Introduction to Part D

Suffering has always been a part of our human condition. No members of the human race have been spared suffering and pain, disease and death. The reality of suffering comes to each of us in varied and completely unexpected ways. Some of our sufferings are objectively small, others of much larger and more tragic proportions. Many times, tragedies strike us in ways unforeseen and from events over which we have no control. At other times, we suffer at the hands of other human beings motivated by fear, power, greed, or hatred, the most horrific repercussion of the original sin.

From the earliest days of God's covenant with the Chosen People, the problem of evil has been present: "If God is good and created us in the image of goodness, then why evil? Why do people suffer? Why do bad things happen to good people?" In the Book of Job, we find an early but timeless wrestling with this problem. There simply is no easy answer.

Nonetheless, something within each woman, man, and child refuses to believe that suffering and death are the end. Within each of us is the resistant grace of hope that brings us close to one another in times of tragedy and urges us to join hands with one another to work against the forces of evil. Evil and suffering do their work in our world, but the gift of hope is equally at our command.

A decision for Christ must result in a decision to live and work for justice and peace in a world where suffering and pain are our constant companions. Pope Paul VI remarked, "If you want peace, then work for justice." We do not know why tragedy strikes our world and our life. We do know that we are called to respond in the most graced and appropriate way possible. That response is the life of compassion.

Compassion is not a weak virtue. Compassion is the commitment to be humanely and deeply present to a person who is in pain. Compassion is the commitment to work, in diverse ways, for the end to every form of oppression and slavery. Compassion is the necessary no to evil and a profound yes to life and freedom. In its purest linguistic roots, it means "to suffer with" those in pain, to suffer with the enigma of suffering itself, to suffer with our human impatience for a new day of peace.

Lesbigay believers have had our share of suffering and tragedy. In decade after decade, movements of fear and ignorance led to our being denied employment, personal liberties, housing, and medical care. Some of us have been beaten, mugged, or even murdered simply for being who we are.

Faith in Christ can motivate us with an inner strength and hope that can heal our bodily and spiritual wounds. The hope of Christ within us calls us to go beyond our present pain, to suffer with it, and to become whole and living human beings. Ultimately, our experience of suffering can make us capable of being present to others who suffer. Especially in these days of the AIDS pandemic, we can be special sources of grace to those who are living with this disease. Bringing compassionate hope is our essential way of life as believers. Finally, hope and compassion are the necessary food and drink that sustain us on our pilgrim way until that day when each of us as equal sisters and brothers are brought to God's peace where every tear will be wiped away.

1
Bearing Others' Fears

Presence | Recall the loving presence of God.

Reflection | Suffering is a part of our history and our experience. The greatest human minds always have questioned why tragedies befall us. As in the Book of Job, we are simply left with the impression that suffering just "is." In the lesbigay community, the image of the leper endures in those who are touched by AIDS. The person with AIDS struggles against misunderstanding, shame, and sometimes a merciless internal self-recrimination. In a sense, the person with AIDS stands again at the door of "coming out." The fear of rejection, persecution, an utter lack of love haunts her or him. People with AIDS need an accepting and empathetic ministry from others as a sign of God's presence and compassion. Tragically, this need has often been unmet. In this time of prayer, we pray for all those who have AIDS or those who are HIV positive, their families and loved ones, and for those who minister to them as the hands of a God whose divine name is Compassion.

Canticle | *Non Serviam?*

Crucified against an alleyway amber
Arms stretched out
blackened by a fear most people leave unnamed
Eyes clenched shut blinded by questions
His throat, twisted in cry:
"Can you love me knowing of this animal
that massacres and feeds upon my dreams day and night?"
I was caught
his question sucking breath out of me
paralyzing me frozen
probing to see if my arms were wide enough
my soul large enough
my loving strong enough

to stay for long beside his wood-pinned life
to listen to his shrieking abandonment
the kind of despair
that common ears hear only as silence or whispers without
      meaning
yet the kind of despair that, for gentler, less-common ears
screams soul-to-soul and makes your hair to stand on end.
From behind his closed eyelids
dark eyes glared at me wondering
eyes in which the alleyway amber
paled before his rage and fear.
This was no devil
no actor caught up in hysteria to move the crowds.
This was simply a man like any other
but a man for whom the accidents of life
had dealt one card too many from the risk-pile.
Suddenly I was aware of ancient legions
seeing a vision of a blood-bathed body
that lately had cried out:
"Why have you abandoned me?"
I saw their knees grow stiff and their spirits stiffer still.
I heard their words: *"Non serviam."* . . . "I will not serve."
And then I knew that in the end
this was an even greater treason
this doing the wrong thing for any reason
this lack of soul, this lack of human trust
this failure to love enough
this running from the human mirror
in which even God had seen himself
and loved it all the more.
Hands then touched like flint, tears flowed warmly.
And in the silence of the night
the alleyway amber dimmed
and hope was kindled in a human spark.

Psalm 41

Reading

From ancient times, you bid us, O God, to look with love
upon those who are poor and who are needy. You extend
your hand to those whose lives are caught up in terror and
despair. To those who hunger, you sustain with love those
who search for the crumbs that might fall from our tables,
for the droplets that may escape our greedy lips and fall like
life itself down to the floor beneath our banquet tables.

When we are sick, you send the moments of comfort that keep us strong to battle our illnesses. Yes, I have sinned against you. Yes, my life hardly mirrors your perfection. I have enemies. They look upon me in my sickness, and they gloat over me. They amuse themselves and snidely wonder when I will die. They speak in whispers to each other that some deadly thing has fastened itself upon me and that I will never again be strong in the sunlight. Even my friend who ate my bread and shared my cup has scorned me and left me alone and lonely. Yet you are my Trusted Friend. You alone stand beside me with your strength. You sustain me and love me. In this I know that you vindicate me with your Presence. I give you thanks forever and will praise your name through all generations.

Intercessions

God stands close to the brokenhearted and never leaves us victims to our despair. Trusting always in the God who suffers with us, we pray: God of life, to you we pray.
- For all those who have AIDS, their families and loved ones, let us pray . . .
- For those who minister to AIDS patients or those who are HIV positive, let us pray . . .
- For all people who suffer from illness, that through our hands they may come to know the comforting presence of a healing God, let us pray . . .
- For all those who serve in health care, that their efforts may end in the successful elimination of every epidemic that mars the beauty of human hope, let us pray . . .
- And for our individual needs . . . , let us pray . . .

Closing

God of all healing, from the dawn of creation our lives have been touched by sickness and dying. Never willing us to be left alone, you send us your love and comfort by our presence to one another. In the fullness of time, you sent to us our Savior, whose Resurrection became our doorway to life immortal. In a particular way, look upon those who live with AIDS and HIV. Look upon any of your children whose sickness brings them to the door of death. Cover them all with the hope of Christ. Bring to them and to all people your gift of healing love that alone can survive the terror of the night and lying whispers of death's finality. We ask this as all things through Christ in the unity of the Holy Spirit, with you, one God, forever and ever. Amen.

The Lord's Prayer. Abba in heaven, your name is holy! Your justice come, your will be done, on earth as in the heavens. Fill us this day with all that we need. Teach us to heal as you have healed us. Bring us not to the test, but deliver us always from the power of evil. You alone are God, and all belongs to you!

2
Suffering Rejection

| Recall the loving presence of God.

Reflection | Rejections are never easy. In fact, they can be the most devastating experiences of our life. They are particularly painful when they come at the hands of those we had called friends. Sometimes rejections come for reasons not of our own fault. We may experience rejection for the values we hold, the lifestyles we espouse, the commitments that we have made, or the persons that we are. Jesus himself suffered great rejection, and ultimately was spurned and killed by the powers of his age. Christians, because of our values and commitments, have often followed Jesus and suffered cruel rejection.

For lesbigay believers, rejection can become almost a way of life. Society's unfounded fears and stereotypes can create a climate of apprehension where the most trusted friends, family members, and associates of lesbigays will turn their back on us. However, a willingness to endure and our praying for the grace of the Holy Spirit in such times are a gift and witness of the courage of disciples of Jesus to stand up for the truth about God: that God never rejects any of us, but embraces us without conditions.

Canticle | **Friend No More**

With the sound of expectant mockery,
the telephone in my office sneered.
It was the voice of a hoped for new friend
asking for a word of conversation.
Something in my soul stirred uneasily.
Something in my expectations
knew that something was not aright.
There was no gladness in his voice.
Missing was the welcome warmth
of friends in conversation.

He needed information,
the kind of information only passed between souls,
the kind of information certainly not passed
at usual times such as these.
But the need for information
did not know the boundaries of commonplace sense.
His fears could not wait. His question was simple.
He needed to know if my life's loves were singed
by that love whose name is dared not spoken.
I was caught:
between commonplace sense
and the place of courage that is the rock of friendship.
How do you respond
when asked to speak your name
and you know that your answer
is poised between politics and courage,
between hell's hiding and heaven's justice?
I answered in courage, slowly and with deliberation.
We spoke of my singed soul.
My soul was singing not singed.
My soul was free; his, was not.
And then he told me there would be no more conversations.
He could not let others know
that we were friends.
He seemed startled that my soul was open to the world.
For him, work and world and Word could not meet.
There could be no Truth about me in his life.
And without Truth, there can be no friends,
no love that draws its life from God.
Perhaps there was some victory for a fragile heart
and the Garden's snake could hide again under its rock.
The line went dead. The moment and the conversation over—
forever.
And at first I was sad.
And then extraordinarily glad.
For the telephone could sneer no more.

Mark 14:66–72

Reading

They had arrested Jesus. He was being condemned at that
very hour. It was a lonely night with no hope of getting any
friendlier. Peter, special friend of the rabbi, was outside the
court in the cold, night air. Soldiers and serving girls out by

the fire tried to warm themselves. Peter inched his way closer to the fire hoping to remain hidden, but he was a large man and difficult to hide even in a crowd. Seeing him crowd himself next to the firepit, one of the serving girls looked up. She scrutinized his face for what seemed a long time, then suddenly announced to the group that this man must be one of that rabbi's friends. She was sure of it. Her announcement caught the attention of everyone standing there. Peter heatedly denied knowing who this Jesus was, and then he slipped away, hoping to melt into the shadows. But she followed him and told another small group of night-dwellers that this man was surely one of the companions of Jesus. Peter denied ever knowing Jesus and nervously sidled away again. By now, the serving girl's accusation had caught the attention of another group. They too questioned Peter, who denied it all in nervous fear. As dawn was breaking, a barnyard rooster crowed. The third crowing pierced Peter's ears and soul. He flinched his head and remembered the words that Jesus said at their final meal. Then Peter ran into the night with tears furrowing his face.

Intercessions

Our life is often marked with the pain of rejection and misunderstanding. Confident that God stands closest to those who suffer unjustly at the hands of others, we pray: God of life, to you we pray.

- For all Christians, that the grace of the Holy Spirit may give us the courage to withstand the pain of rejection for our love of mercy and goodness, let us pray . . .
- For living martyrs for the cause of justice and peace, let us pray . . .
- For lesbigays everywhere who suffer rejection at the hands of friends, family, and associates, that the spirit of justice and forgiveness may be our gift in return, let us pray . . .
- For all who turn away from any other person for reasons contrary to human understanding or the cause of the Gospel, let us pray . . .
- And for our individual needs . . . , let us pray . . .

Closing

O God, source of all love, despite the beauty and goodness with which you have created us, we have permitted the power of evil to turn us from mutual affection and to make us servants of enmity. Cast out all fears and hatreds. In the spirit of Christ Jesus, teach us to loosen our fists, and to make of our hands bridges of welcome for all people. We ask this, as all things, through Christ in the unity of the Holy Spirit, with you, one God, forever and ever. Amen.

The Lord's Prayer. Abba in heaven, your name is holy! Your justice come, your will be done, on earth as in the heavens. Fill us this day with all that we need. Teach us to heal as you have healed us. Bring us not to the test, but deliver us always from the power of evil. You alone are God, and all belongs to you!

3
Victims Never Again

Presence | Recall the loving presence of God.

Reflection | At the end of the 1940s, the world became painfully more aware of the horrors perpetrated by the Nazi regime on our Jewish sisters and brothers, on gypsies, the mentally ill, gay persons, and a host of other subgroupings in the European population during World War II. The horrifying pictures of mass graves and dead bodies from the crematoria burned into the consciousness of the world. We still face these grim pictures of brutality and are reminded never to forget how we are capable of making victims of one another.

Victimization finds its origins in hatred, bigotry, exploitative power, and the desire for domination. And victimization has yet to be eradicated in our own time. In the promises of baptism, Christians pledge themselves to fight ceaselessly to end every form of power that makes victims of any human being. The victimization of lesbigays is well documented and is as senseless as any other form of power that robs persons of life, liberty, and equal rights. However, for those who have been victims or those who are touched by the tragedy of victimization, the appropriate response is to work for the end of hate, bigotry, fear, and brutality. To do so puts flesh on our verbal commitment that we reverence the God whose first tabernacle is our human community and each of its members.

Canticle | ## Job's Mound

Like a room full of polite folk who lately heard an improperty,
it seemed the whole universe around me was holding its breath
waiting for a reply to my sudden revelation.

Nothing could seem more pregnant or more feared,
nothing could counter the dread anticipation
after my words had filled the air
and my soul felt torn in two
like a curtain ripped apart
opening up to the mockery of everyone
the loving secret of my spirit
that had chased me up and down the pathways
of all the years of my existence.
Months ago, tragedy had struck.
A full-throated, unrelated lie
born of some unknown and undeserved malignancy.
Fearful that my real secret would be discovered,
I had sunk my sorrows into a deeper lie,
a bottled anesthesia,
that robbed me of any necessary strength.
The daily round of drink and pills
had done, as promised, nothing more
than rob me of my soul
and of my resolve to fight that horrid nightmare
with strong grace and utter truth.
The lie was finally forsaken.
But the aftermath of wounds and tears
could not so easily be erased
by simple words of apology.
The damage had been complete
and demanded a deeper healing
that takes the time of one's life
and makes it into something more.
Now no more was there that daily obsession
to wash away my angers with madness and resentment.
Months had gone by and my soul was revealed to me,
the inner grace that God had given me
as utter gift.
No longer could I resist the gift of truth.
Now, with those to whom my care had been given,
I was invited to reveal the inner recesses of my soul.
And so I did.
I took the leap of faith that I had feared.
I spoke of that love that often dares not speak its own name.
And I looked and waited . . . and waited.
Slowly, the words formed on his lips in reply.
And I saw the sneering demon of abandonment
rear its ugly head in laughter.

I was told, "No more."
"No more can you walk with us."
"No more can you live among us."
"You are something unclean."
Inside me something like brittle glass heaved under the
    strain.
Anticipation gave way to what had been anticipated.
The fever was broken. Fears were met.
I had been waiting
and indeed the other shoe had dropped.
All the riches and dreams of years gone by
were seemingly gone forever in a deft blow
of simple words that made me sit upon a dunghill.
Some invisible hand grabbed the back of my neck
and seemed to squeeze the life from my mind.
A fog enveloped me as if to protect me from what was said.
I was numb
a confusing mass of rage and indignation
of fear and sadness
clutched the most private parts of my being.
I was alone.
Nothing more could be done.
I bowed my head knowing there was nothing left.
I had spoken my inner name.
I had laid my heart open.
And it had been ravaged.
Like Job, I felt I lost the sons and daughters of my life,
the fleeting successes and pleasures
that had seemed to give me meaning.
All now was gone. Never to return.
I rose from my chair in utter disbelief.
I was left without words.
I made my way to a small chapel.
And there in the midst of dim candle flickers
I bowed my head and heard those ancient words
arise from my own lips:
"The Lord gives and the Lord takes away.
Blessed be the name of the Lord."

Reading | Acts 7:54—8:3

When the high priest and the full council of the people's
elders heard Stephen's words, they were filled with rage and
anger. They shouted insults and blasphemies at him, even

grinding their teeth and raising their fists. The place broke
out into pandemonium, a near riot. But Stephen, filled
with an abundance of grace, raised his head toward heaven.
His face became radiant as he saw the Risen Christ standing
at the right hand of God coming toward him. Stephen ex-
claimed to the rioting elders and those gathered, "Look, I see
the Son of Man in all glory standing at the right hand of our
Abba." The gathered crowd would not hear of it. They covered their ears and shouted so as to drown out the truth of
Stephen's words. Eventually, they could not stand his peace-
ful presence any longer. As one body, they rose up, laid violent hands on him, and dragged him by his hair and clothing
to the edge of the city. No longer able to hold back their
rage, they hurled stones at Stephen. To make their stoning
more effective, they took off their outer garments and
laid them at the feet of one Saul of Tarsus who stood there
gloating at what he thought was a victory. But Stephen did
nothing more than pray. The radiance of his soul shone out.
Joining his life to the Christ, Stephen gave up his spirit as he
whispered his final words, "Jesus, receive my spirit. Do not
hold this sin against them." With that he died. Saul approved
of the murder. That same day, riots broke out, and Saul led
the way for the murder of other innocents whose only crime
was the love of Christ. Many were committed to prison and
others killed.

Intercessions

In every age, the martyrs have given their lives for the dignity of the human family and the truth of the Gospel. That we
may be inspired by them to work for justice and peace, we
pray: God of life, to you we pray.
- For all who have been made victims in our world for the
  sake of justice and peace, let us pray . . .
- For those who persecute others or who deprive others of
  life, dignity, and equal rights, that they may be converted
  from violence to peace, let us pray . . .
- For an end to bigotry, hatred, and discrimination in every
  form, let us pray . . .
- For the members of the lesbigay family, especially those
  who have been made victims of human discrimination,
  let us pray . . .
- And for our individual needs . . . , let us pray . . .

Closing | O God, you placed within us a hunger and thirst for love and peace. Yet the power of evil has sown the maddening seeds of hatred and fear. In Christ, you have called us to put aside hatred. You bid us cast out from our midst all things that mar the beauty of your world. Convert our heart so that we may never again raise our hands against one another. We ask this as all things through Christ in the unity of the Holy Spirit, with you, one God, forever and ever. Amen.

The Lord's Prayer. Abba in heaven, your name is holy! Your justice come, your will be done, on earth as in the heavens. Fill us this day with all that we need. Teach us to heal as you have healed us. Bring us not to the test, but deliver us always from the power of evil. You alone are God, and all belongs to you!

4
Embracing Sorrows

Recall the loving presence of God.

Among the many expressions of compassion, learning to be present to a suffering person has to be one of the most difficult interpersonal skills to learn. Many of us are taught subconsciously that every problem must have a solution and quick resolution. Nevertheless, human life is not quite that easy. The ills that plague us, whether individually or socially, do not lend themselves to swift and uncomplicated solutions. As one bright college student remarked once, "It makes no sense to try and solve anyone else's problems; what makes most sense is learning to be present to their pain."

Christian believers reverence the image of the Mother of Jesus and others who attended to Christ on the cross without being able to "solve" the situation. We learn how to be present to someone else in pain when we learn to be present to "the pain within." Members of the lesbigay community who have learned to touch and be transfigured by their pain receive an invitation to a deeper sense of compassion for others. Lesbigay believers can be wonderful witnesses of Christ's compassion—"suffering with"—to people in the most painful moments of their life.

Stabat Mater

Fingers slowly rolling the rosary in my pocket,
I stepped onto the escalator to go a flight below
and catch the metro in a kind of pilgrim way.
It was a short trip when calculating by a clock;
a much longer trip when you try and fathom
how a nation could take this long, tortured route
to forgetfulness.
Today, the green span of a nation's mall was broken into
     pieces
with the quilt-stitched witness of a million hopes and fears.

As if muted in the moment, my quarters mutely fell.
I took my ticket and mounted into a mute metro.
It seemed, from my heart's eye, that all the world had fallen
        mute.
Women and men, so many bearing a telltale ribbon,
with serious resolve headed together to the nation's mall.
A short ride.
But almost interminable.
How did we ever get to this place?
Here indeed is a pilgrim way, some stations of another cross.
I left the metro and went up the escalator
to emerge into a mass of human sorrows, angers, and hopes.
Thousands, it seemed millions, stunned into silence,
remembering this place like another Gettysburg
where the slain, the victims of a newer dread war,
were victims yet again
of wagging tongues and self-righteous accusations
of a world that all too often looks for scapegoats.
The silent whispers of the crowd were echoed in their slow
        footfalls:
the scuff and shuffle of the mourning,
the lost, the curious, and the chastened.
In the breeze of this afternoon, for a seeming eternal
        moment,
those who were accusers no longer washed their hands like
        Pilate
but seemed embraced in love's compassion
with those who grieved the passing of these too-many.
My rosary warmed in lockstep
with the warmth of tears across my cheeks.
At once, my head looked up in answer
to a sound of louder whimpers.
There before me, my eyes were arrested at a sight of tender
        love
not easily dismissed by dim eyes and dimmer minds.
Before one of the panels, an older woman and a younger man
were locked arm-in-arm into an embrace,
rocking each other tenderly.
No words, just a steady stream of tears.
An occasional, glazed look beyond themselves
recalled again by some sharp memory no longer of this life.
There before me:
a sorrowful mother
a beloved.

Gathered again at another cross, another Calvary.
Another mother who did not understand and had questioned.
Yet another mother who had remained faithful even in her
     doubts,
her human questions tempered in a mother's trusting.
Another beloved who had heard something true
and had followed in love even to the bitter end.
There they stood at the foot of another cross, a cross of quilt,
not fixed by nails and thorn scrapes,
but fixed with stitches that spoke all the memories
     and sorrows,
all the fears and hopes of those who longed for justice and
     peace,
the end of our inhumanity to each other.
There in this scene, where centuries and faith were spanned,
another mother had found another son, another home;
another son had found another mother, another loving.
A silent voice from the cross-quilt gives them now to one
     another.
And the crisp air seemed to reach down deep inside my
     pilgrim-soul
and made old words come new:
"At the cross their station keeping
stood they gently ever weeping,
close to Jesus to the last."

John 19:25–30   Reading

They had taken Jesus and had crucified him with two others.
Indeed, they seemed to have split his life in two. They also
rent his garments and cast lots for the pieces, especially for
his seamless cloth. Nothing was sacred to them. Everything
was a source of scorn and profit. Jesus was not left alone,
however. A faithful few stayed close to his place of execution.
His mother was there. So too were his mother's sister and
others of the women. Among these faithful also was that one
disciple who was most beloved by Jesus. Weary and bloodied
even on his throne of offering, Jesus saw his mother and the
beloved disciple. How much more could he give them? Despite the risk, they had followed him in his worst hour even
to this grim moment. He said to his mother, "This now is
your son." And to the beloved disciple, "This now is your
mother." They had come to him and had stood close. Now he
gave them to each other in love. Knowing that everything
then was in order and that his life, his presence on the earth,

had been brought to completion, he was thirsty and drank from the common wine that they held up on a sponge to dull his pain. He smiled, looked out at the whole world that he loved, and said, "It is finished." Bowing his head, he breathed forth his legacy.

Intercessions

The God of our faith is always present to us, carrying us in a special, tender way especially when we suffer. That we may learn to be as present to one another as God is to us, we pray: God of life, to you we pray.

- For all those who suffer, that the presence of God may be manifest to them in the care that comes from human friendship and compassion, let us pray . . .
- For those who fear the sorrows of others and run from those who are most in need, that God may convert our fears into the courage to be of service to the suffering, let us pray . . .
- For all those who suffer in silence and in abandonment, that God may move us to seek them out and be present to them, let us pray . . .
- For lesbigay believers, that our compassion may be a gift from our community to all the world, let us pray . . .
- And for our individual needs . . . , let us pray . . .

Closing

O God of all life, in Christ you walked among us, embracing our joys and our sorrows, our hopes and our fears. In this earthly pilgrimage, the suffering of your people cries out to heaven. Teach us to move beyond our fears and to open our hands and heart to those who suffer. Help us to give healing to the wounds of others and to embrace those who suffer grief and loneliness. In Christ, teach us to love one another as you have loved us. We ask this, as all things, through Christ in the unity of the Holy Spirit, with you, one God, forever and ever. Amen.

The Lord's Prayer. Abba in heaven, your name is holy! Your justice come, your will be done, on earth as in the heavens. Fill us this day with all that we need. Teach us to heal as you have healed us. Bring us not to the test, but deliver us always from the power of evil. You alone are God, and all belongs to you!

5
From Death to Life

Recall the loving presence of God.

Presence

When we watch the nightly news, violence and crime invade
our homes. Whenever we pick up a newspaper, we cannot
help but see how violence is a part of our world. Nowhere
can we run to avoid the bitter truth that the forces of death
are present and working among us to the destruction of
lives, property, human dignity, and the glory of creation.

Reflection

   In the Gospel portraits, Jesus confronted the powers of
death and destruction. In Christ's death, God suffered with
the tragedies of human violence and unjust murder. As disciples of Jesus, Christians are called to confront violence and
death with courage. Every time that Christians confront war,
destruction, crime, murder, and oppression, we are called to
counter these forces with the message of the cross and the
Resurrection. As with all Christians, lesbigay believers must
do the same. As members of a community that has seen our
sisters and brothers treated violently simply for being different, we are especially called to attend the needs of the suffering, actively work for the end of such senseless brutalities,
and be messengers of stalwart hope. In short, lesbigay wom-
en and men of faith are called to stand at the tombs of the
murdered and with every ounce of human strength preach
"Christ" against any force that would deprive anyone of life,
dignity, and freedom.

Station XIV

Canticle

An eerie chalk outline, bonelike and stark upon the
      pavement,
seemed to have been etched by some accusing finger
as if to encircle the whole history of the world's hatreds
within a few square feet of one night's passing glance.

Like the gaping, silent mouth of a broken statue,
the perimeter of a body once filled with life,
but lately snuffed out,
screaming broke the clocked routine of my day.
The mottled pavement within the outline
was broken only by a dried blood stain
that oozed into the memories of passersby
if they dared to care.
Another silent victim to the screaming rage of ignorance
that boils within each age's tyrants
who would rather kill than take the time
to know the meaning of another soul.
What might have happened?
Were there words that sparked a conflict?
What city-street challenge could be the cause
of a murder in this place?
Next to the chalk outline, so reminiscent of a skeleton,
were simple words written by some angry hand:
"Another bashing, another murder. When will IT stop?"
I closed my eyes and was whisked back over the centuries
to a hill of murders and a garden of resting.
A chalky outline of a tomb, newly carved,
in which no corpse had yet been placed,
was being prepared for another Victim
another Son slain for his difference.
The words he spoke and the life he led
were such a cause for conflict
in city streets and temple precincts.
The bone-white winding sheets in which they carried him
were stained red with his oozing blood.
Perhaps in the face of his mother and his friends
the question "When will IT stop?" was framed then as now.
But IT has never stopped for we never let IT:
Abel's blood crying out to heaven.
Rachel weeping for her children are "no more."
The slain innocents cindered in the Holocaust.
Slave masses killed by white-robed cross-burning bigots.
Martyrs for justice of every age and every nation.
Each and every one of these
now joined at this sidewalk pavement of a bashing-tomb
     to ask:
"When will IT stop?"

But we never let our apathy turn blood-raged at spilt blood.
We cannot answer and thus will be made to answer
for our silence,
which makes us partners
to the death march and the killing.
Oh, that I could hear that Ancient Echo now:
"Why do you look for the Living among the dead?"
Oh, that I could have the courage
to look inside myself and find the murderer, the IT,
that bashes and kills the children of the earth.
Now, in silence, I pray
and ask the God of justice to make me merciful
and find it in my heart to stop the killer there
that killing everywhere might have an end.
Here, in this chalky sidewalk outline of a tomb
with its blood-stained center and its eerie, probing question;
here we have laid Him to rest
and await always the power of His Rising.

Luke 23:50–56

Reading

He was dead. There was no question. Even the soldiers had
left the scene convinced that his execution, more aptly his
murder, was completed. The air was still and the smell of
death was everywhere. His body was lifeless, bloodless, and
limp upon the wood of his sentencing. The small, white sign
that had proclaimed his crime at the top of the wooden stake
was creaking in the small breezes. Joseph of Arimathea, a
very good man, had arranged with Pilate for a hasty but
appropriate burial in a new tomb according to Jewish cus-
tom. It was late on the day of preparation. Everything had to
be completed swiftly. Other details could be taken care of on
Sunday morning after the passing of this special Sabbath. So
they took his body down from the cross and laid it in the
arms of the women who were with the party. Perhaps his
mother was among them. It was unclear. Regardless of who
actually was there, Jesus' friends carried his body in new
cloths. His corpse was an eerie gray against the white, fresh
linens that were becoming his shroud. Odd how the bleak
colors that shadowed his figure mirrored the hopelessness
and sorrow that had invaded those who were there. After his
agony, they laid him to rest in that new tomb. And then they
themselves went off to their Sabbath rest, wondering what
the future might hold for each of them now that he was
dead.

Intercessions Faced as we are with the full story of human life and death, believers of every time and place are called to bring the message of the crucified and risen Christ even where the powers of death are most in evidence. That we may be faithful witnesses always and everywhere, we pray: God of life, to you we pray.

- For all those who are victims of murder and crime, that Christ may enfold them into his peace in a special way, let us pray . . .
- For those who suffer from the tragic loss of loved ones and friends, that the consoling Spirit may be present to them in their confusion and their pain, let us pray . . .
- For all Christians, that we may work tirelessly for an end to every form of human violence, and for the conversion of the violent themselves, let us pray . . .
- For the members of our lesbigay community who have lost their life at the hands of the violent, that they may know the peace of God and that their death may move us to rid our society of every form of bigotry and hatred, let us pray . . .
- And for our individual needs . . . , let us pray . . .

Closing O God, indeed you weep at the tragic deaths of your children. Like Rachel and the women of Bethlehem who wailed over the slaughter of the innocents, your heart breaks and your voice cries out through all the universe when one of your children is cut down by hatred and discrimination. In Christ, teach us to cry out with you and to work for your justice until that day when every form of human violence is wiped from the face of the earth and when every oppressor is converted to your path of peace and gentle goodness. We ask this, as all things, through Christ in the unity of the Holy Spirit, with you, one God, forever and ever. Amen.

The Lord's Prayer. Abba in heaven, your name is holy! Your justice come, your will be done, on earth as in the heavens. Fill us this day with all that we need. Teach us to heal as you have healed us. Bring us not to the test, but deliver us always from the power of evil. You alone are God, and all belongs to you!

"everytime you wash and love each other ~ i will be with you"

John 13: 1-20

Part E

Handing on the Message of Courage:
Called to the Service of Justice and Peace

Introduction to Part E

John Donne's words, no person "is an island," have been quoted time and time again. Perhaps the human race should have taken greater notice of Donne's words when the industrialization of society, the great political revolutions, and the advances of technology led to unhealthy individualism in the West. Contemporary humanists, philosophers, and social scientists remind us that the great discoveries of the modern era have exacted a price.

Particularly in the United States, a type of easy individualism and any number of demographic changes fostered a shift in the way we unconsciously see ourselves in relationship to one another, our world, and all of creation. Many modern commentators urge us to revisit less technological times and cultures to reclaim the sense of grassroots community and human contingency.

Human beings, by our very nature, are incomplete. We must rely upon the world and others to satisfy the most basic and most profound of our needs. None of us can live without food and drink or shelter. None of us can remain healthily alive without self-esteem and love and beauty. Deep within us, we know the truth of all this.

And yet we fear being vulnerable by having someone else help us or helping someone else. Human service, the ability to be servant or steward for someone else, is uncomfortable and can make many demands. The act of letting ourselves be helped is equally disconcerting as we must resign our mad attempts to control or be in power. Contingent as we are, this is the sum and substance of our life: we live and move and have our being in a God who has decidedly placed us in this world together.

Throughout the Judeo-Christian tradition, all statements of faith entail the demand to be of service to God and neighbor. In fact, the Scriptures remind us vividly that the presence of God is to be found within each human being and within all of creation's story. To claim a lively faith in Jesus Christ is not to escape from a life of commitment to the world and its needs. Though we may believe completely in life after this life, we are called to live within the present world and to work for the betterment of all life through responsible personal lifestyles, political and societal commitments based on justice, and daily relationships with every other human being marked by love, compassion, unselfishness, and peace.

Lesbigay believers are called to this same sense of Christian service. Like those faithful disciples hidden in the fear of that upper room, we have often learned how to care for one another without discrimination. The injustices and fears that we have experienced can become a motivation to help all those in need. By listening to another person who is slowly coming to own their inner identity, feeding the sick, burying the dead, working on a soup line, helping a company shape business policies that are more just, offering our giftedness to our churches, simply being a good neighbor in our local communities, we make a positive contribution to the human family like every other good member of society. We are called like everyone else to join in the task of building a better society where every person is valued and treated as the presence of Christ. From our own deprivations and sad experiences to our enduring hope purified by the fire of our life and aspirations, we are joined with every woman, man, and child to tend the garden of God's delights that is this Eden we call Earth.

1
The Cries of the Poor

Presence | Recall the loving presence of God.

Reflection | Serving other people is seldom convenient. Despite the romance permeating pious stories of faith, the service of others more often happens in ways that are discomforting to us. Perhaps the invitation to service comes at an hour inconvenient to our personal or work schedules. Perhaps those who come to us in need are people whose background or character disturb our pretenses or our sensibilities. Perhaps the service asked for occasions fear, anger, or a feeling of being inept.

Whatever the case may be, the invitation of Christ for us to serve our sisters and brothers always exacts some price and offers promise. In Christ, God entered into the world and inconveniently loved us. Jesus touched the outcast, the poor, the possessed, the despised, the irascible, even members of his society who were hated because they were aligned with Roman colonial rule. Jesus freely entered the areas of human disease, poverty, shame, and death. Nothing escaped his touch and his love. Certainly, being crucified was not a convenient form of loving us. In Christ, all disciples of Jesus are called to do the same. We are called to give of what has been given us. Lesbigays are reminded to give from the loving abundance that others have given to us when we suffered. Together with all believers, we are meant to have open ears and open hearts to hear the cries of the poor and touch them in loving care no matter how inconvenient the call, no matter how distasteful the task.

Canticle | ## Open Air Mandatum

With a spring wind hurrying me along,
I moved down the street of the inner city
to meet with friends and speak together
about our lives
which previously had been held in liquid bondage.

The sounds of Easter shoppers broke the air:
voices filled with something new, something like spring.
There was a freshness everywhere except one:
inside me.
Inside me were all the things that one would expect
from a self-imposed tomb
of bitterness and resentment.
Angers without names
made me resent even the springtime
and the beauty of changing seasons
and human joy and laughter.
This was the night
supposedly different from any other night.
The night that Christians held sacred
as the beginning of their festival of freedom.
Each year before, I spent this night in prayer
entering into the mysteries of death and of life.
It was a night to wash feet, to share food and cup,
to be forgiven and raised up.
But this year, my shadow would grace no church door.
Anger withheld my footsteps from finding my way to God.
This year I was doing just my duty to stay sober
and then off to dancing with friends
in our secret places,
places safe from a bashing world.
No church this year. This year, only life.
My life, such as it was.
I hurried down the street into center city
letting the hands of bitterness cover the ears of my heart.
But my eyes stayed open.
And across the way from me,
I saw something curious and frightening all at once.
An old man on a subway grate covered with homelessness.
A younger man crouching near him, but not too closely
careful not to catch whatever ailed the man.
The elder babbled about someone named Joe.
I hurried over, asking if there was anything I could do:
hoping I had stopped some insane prank
that might have been a harm to the older man.
Sopped up with liquor, he still was able to ask:
"Have ya seen, Joe?"
"Man, am I hungry! Get me somethin' to eat and drink?"
Almost without thinking, I went to the store across the street.
Styrofoamed coffee and a stale pastry.

I went back.
The older man was still babbling his story to the younger.
Still mouthing his broken dreams and unreal hopes
from his generation to another.
I looked him straight into his dazed and dirt-ringed eyes.
He smiled.
And the hair on the back of my neck stood up.
Story and hopes.
Broken dreams and bridges between disparate generations.
Food and drink and hands offering and receiving.
Holy Thursday on a subway grate.
An open air Mandatum.
And then I knew,
and my resentments melted in the springtime air.
Something clean was happening around me, in me.
I would not go in to God.
And so God came out to me.
And once again familiar words were voiced anew:
"If I who am your Lord and Master do this for you,
then do the same for one another."

Reading | John 13:1–20

The air was filled with something that could not be named.
Tomorrow the lambs would be slaughtered in anticipation of
the Passover. Tonight, we were seated with him at table in a
meal of friendship. We often had such meals. But there was
something discernibly different in the air this time, as if
something new and unprecedented was about to happen.
Without a word, he looked at each of us in turn. It felt as if
he were looking right through each person at the table.
Then, he left his place, put on the servant's apron, and began
to wash our feet with the ewer and basin prepared for this
task that was normally the work of slaves. Astonishing. The
rabbi was washing our feet. I felt my toes curl up. My legs
wanted to shrivel into my body at the very thought of his
touching me in the way that slaves do. He went around the
table and washed each person's feet in turn. Simon made
quite a scene, to which Jesus simply shook his head slowly
and made that curious smile whenever Simon made an em-
barrassment of himself. In the end, we all were washed.
When it was over, Jesus addressed what he did. "Do you see
what I have done for you? You call me your Lord. And yet I
did not hesitate to wash your feet. Do the same for each

other. You call me your Master. And yet I have always loved you. Do the same. This is the way I wish you to remember me. For every time you wash and love each other, I will be with you." As usual, his words sounded strange and caught my soul somewhere between flying and hiding. That was the way things always ended when the Teacher made a point. It was as if he raised more questions than we asked for.

In Christ, God has taught us that our common bond with one another is loving service of all people and especially of the poor. That we may have the courage to love without counting the cost, we pray: Hear and answer, tender God. | **Intercessions**
- For all Christians, that we may make the concerns of the poor and the needy our daily bread, let us pray . . .
- For those who dedicate their life to the ministries of social justice, let us pray . . .
- For those whose ears are deaf to the poor and whose eyes are blind to the needs of the many, that Jesus might lead them to a lively concern for all in need, let us pray . . .
- For lesbigay believers everywhere, that Christ, God-with-us, may raise us beyond our concerns so that we may join all our sisters and brothers to feed the poor and the lowly, let us pray . . .
- And for our individual needs . . . , let us pray . . .

O God, in Christ you have taught us to feed one another with the bread of human loving and to make the needs of the lowly our own. Help us to give generously to those more in need than ourselves. Open our ears to hear the cries of the poor until that day when all people shall be called to your eternal banquet and every hunger and thirst shall be satisfied. We ask this, as all things, through Christ in the unity of the Holy Spirit, with you, one God, forever and ever. Amen. | **Closing**

The Lord's Prayer. Abba in heaven, your name is holy! Your justice come, your will be done, on earth as in the heavens. Fill us this day with all that we need. Teach us to heal as you have healed us. Bring us not to the test, but deliver us always from the power of evil. You alone are God, and all belongs to you!

2
Listening

Presence	Recall the loving presence of God.
Reflection	When we hear the word *ministry*, we can be quite daunted. The word is ordinarily associated with the official service of the Christian churches. However, ministry is the business of every baptized Christian. Though the churches do have official ministries, the act of ministering to others is much broader in scope and definition. Each baptized disciple enters into the royal priesthood of Jesus, the commitment to advance the holiness and life of all people. As Paul reminded the Corinthians, there are many forms of service in the community, but the greatest of all is love.
	Part of loving is learning to have truly open ears and an open heart to those who are suffering. Perhaps someone is filled with confusion and fear. Perhaps another is caught in the grip of resentments. Perhaps yet another has a need to share some story of joy. Whatever the case may be, an important Christian ministry is learning to listen to the stories of our brothers and sisters, listening without judgment, listening with eager anticipation and attentiveness. In the voice of the storyteller, Jesus is speaking to us. Lesbigay believers have their own stories of faith, hope, sadness, joy, and anticipation. Often because no one listened to us at various times in our life or maybe because our stories were mocked, we have been given an extraordinary invitation to listen to others in Christ. Christ speaks, and we listen. And in our listening, people are made more eager for the Word of Life.
Canticle	**Hotline**
	Quickly shaking off wandering thoughts and wonderings, I struggled to open my eyes as the phone screamed at me to pay attention. I hoped this was not another prank,

another feeble and annoying attempt
at adolescent humor.
I was so tempted not to answer,
convinced that what might come across the line
and what might come as my response
would not amount to anything
but remain a useless way to pass another night
better spent in other ways more pleasureful.
Why in the world had I thrown my hat into the ring?
What ever made me think that I could make a difference?
What differences can be made
in answering the indifferent
or offering a professional silence
to snickering and muffled laughter
only to be followed by my hanging up the phone
and wishing that I could hang it up before them in righteous
        rage.
The phone kept screaming.
Do I answer it?
Or do I leave it and wait
for an inevitable silence to fall again,
a silence that blessedly gets mingled
with all the other silences of the night?
Part of my problem is
that I can never leave well enough alone.
Something always seems to tug inside me
to pull me to places where I would rather not go.
Something in me is curious enough to wonder
if there really is a difference I can make.
Perhaps it is a conspiracy of the soul
that sometimes makes me wonder
if the difference I make is nothing more
than the proud posturing of self-importance,
a puffed up adulation of the self,
that comes because it never came before
from the hands of others you wished would give it.
My quick flirtation with self-importance
gave way to the disturbed agitation I often feel
when someone or something disrupts my hazy inner
        slumber.
I reached toward the persistent phone
like a frustrated parent
attempting to muffle an attention-seeking child
whose concerns come before everything else in life.

As if my laziness were a better judgment
than a quick and sharp "hello,"
my hand, almost in boredom,
raised the phone to my ear and I spoke just as boringly:
"Hotline. Can I help you?"
A screaming silence.
A small, broken voice.
A slight implication
of a torrent of human emotion deeper still,
too tentative to let itself be heard:
"I don't want to live.
I don't understand.
Help me."
Something rent my heart into pieces of guilt.
The icy boredom melted around me
into something like shame and fear.
Without any thought at all,
without the premeditation of any learning,
the words just poured out:
"I know. I don't understand either.
But perhaps together we can try."

Reading   ## Psalm 28

O God, foundation of all the earth, do not close your ears to
me. Hear me. Hear the cries of my pleading. Do not let the
sound of my voice echo through the hills and valleys without
an answer. Do not let my cries for your grace go unheeded.
If you do not hear me, if my cries fade into the wind, then
surely I shall be condemned into loneliness. Hear the sounds
of my prayers and my need for your love. I lift up my hands
to you and grasp for your love through the night. Do not
leave me alone, O loving God. The wicked close their ears to
you. Their ears are closed to the cries of the lonely. Their
mocking laughter drowns out the sobs of those who are in
need. The wicked hear nothing but themselves. But you,
O God, are my strength and my stronghold. You are my re-
deemer. You are blessed for you always hear the sound of my
pleading and do not let my voice vanish into the silence of
the night. Therefore, my heart exults in you and my whole
body is made glad. For you hear me and your voice resounds
within me, making me to tremble with joy and love. O God,
you are the strength of your people. You are the refuge of

your anointed. Save your people. Bless those destined to inherit your word. Be our shepherd and carry our groanings in your heart evermore.

God ever hears the sounds of our cries and is attentive to the needs of the poor. That we may hear the needs of others and provide for them, we pray: Hear and answer, tender God.

Intercessions

- For all those who are searching for that gift of human love that makes their stories cherished and nourished in the spirit of friendship, let us pray . . .
- For those who have been abandoned and whose voices have been made silent by the tragedy of human apathy, let us pray . . .
- For all believers, that the Spirit may make our heart more open to hear the needs of those who suffer, let us pray . . .
- For the members of the lesbigay community, as we have known the comfort of God's providence in friendship, may we be generous in our attentive love to those in need, let us pray . . .
- And for our individual needs . . . , let us pray . . .

O God, you always stand close to those whom the world holds in silence. You never forget the lowly and those in need. In Christ you reached into our world and raised up those whose voices had been drowned out. Never let us forget how you have heard our small voices in your love; but, in the power of your spirit, keep our ears ever open to hear the cries of the poor and serve them. We ask this, as all things, through Christ in the unity of the Holy Spirit, with you, one God, forever and ever. Amen.

Closing

The Lord's Prayer. Abba in heaven, your name is holy! Your justice come, your will be done, on earth as in the heavens. Fill us this day with all that we need. Teach us to heal as you have healed us. Bring us not to the test, but deliver us always from the power of evil. You alone are God, and all belongs to you!

3
Mirror Image

Presence | Recall the loving presence of God.

Reflection | Most of us realize that human beings are created good. We wish to be good persons of service to our neighbors and our world. Yet our flight from people who are in need puzzles us. Any number of us can look back over the course of our life and remember instances when we were less than eager to help another person. Perhaps we had a conflict of schedules or of means. However, a gnawing inner truth admits that our flight from others was perhaps fired by something far deeper and more pervasive.

When we look at other people, essentially we are looking into a mirror. We see ourselves in them. That is part of the way we make our friends. We see in them our goodness or the virtue we wish to have. We see in those we dislike and shy away from the very things that we fear within us. They are our shadow-selves.

However, Christians celebrate that in Christ we have been reconciled to God. A strange word *reconciliation*. It comes from the Latin root *cilium* meaning "eyelash." When we are reconciled with God, God and we stand eyelash to eyelash. God sees us intimately and loves us as we are. We see in God's eyes our very selves, our hopes, our fears, our failures, all that we dream we can yet be—and we believe. For believers, and for lesbigay disciples of Jesus particularly, we have a providential opportunity to minister with grace and power when we welcome others into our life precisely because within them we see the totality of our self and we see the totality of the all-accepting Christ. In taking steps toward reconciliation, our valleys are filled, and our hope is born again and again.

Companion

Like the paste-faced hunger of the city's homeless
pressing noses and eyes at the windows of well-lit restaurants
with the hunger steaming up the glass where their lips touch
she sat before me
wondering, waiting with longing
filled with all the human confusion and fumbling
that comes when you look into your own soul
and cannot make sense of the pieces of its puzzle:
looking and longing for something of substance
to still the ravenous hunger of her questions
knowing full well that the answers she feared within her
would mean taking a different fork in the road.
Such a road.
Never before thought, never ever dreamed, only feared.
A road before which she had always stood in absolute terror.
Her mind filled with images of stones and blood
aimed at her, pouring out of her:
the rejection of family and friends
and all those who once had walked with her in delight.
Now, the secret inside her no longer would remain silent
and cried out from deep within her body and spirit
like a new warrior whose name of gentle love
would no longer be kept a prisoner of her rage and
        nightmares.
I listened quietly to the storm that spewed around me,
a hurricane of meaning
garbled in the wake of anticipation
yet pregnant with a deeper living
beyond the death of leaving behind her hiding.
Once, a long time ago, I had stood at this same road-fork.
I knew the buffets and raging winds of fear
that had kept me from taking those first steps.
Then, there was no one to listen,
there was no one with whom to break some bread
and be companion to my nervous pacing
at the starting gate of discovery,
this race with one's self.
In those former days I had stood at a cliff-point
and never could believe that my leap of faith
would end in life and not damnation.
Now, resolved by my memories of my once lonely journey
my own soul can never leave in distress
those who stand at this same brink of their life

and fear that at the bottom of the precipice
no Hands would catch them in their leaping.
She looked at me.
And in that looking I saw behind the mirror of her eyes
all the taunts she had received:
a family, that called her "leper";
women, that called her "traitor";
men, that called her "ungrateful";
friends, that called her "no more";
and holy people, that called her "sin."
Now, between us and around us
there was another Voice,
a Voice that knows the deeper Truth
more deeply than the human mind
which seeks to mount the Tower of Babel in every age
and believe that we set the standards of Truth
by the limits of our fears.
Now, this deeper Voice spoke clearly
within the brief whispers of souls embracing one another;
and in the quiet silence of the moment,
I gently stretched my hands
to touch the tips of her fingers
gnarled around each other.
And in that touching,
bread was broken,
stone-fears ever so slightly cracked,
one leg stirred with trepidation
and together we were stretched
to put one foot forward
and take the first step on that freedom-journey
together.

Reading | 2 Corinthians 5:16–21

From this day forward and forever, we can no longer regard
anyone from the perspective of the powers of the world. For
the powers of the world do not see aright. At one time, we
even viewed Christ from that perspective and did not grasp
the fullness of Christ's power and redemption in our life.
Now we no longer regard Christ in that perspective and
therefore do not regard each other in the same way either.
If anyone is in Jesus, then that person is an utterly new creation. Everything old and fearful has passed away from us
and from within us. There is nothing in us that is not of God.

Nothing at all! All this is from God who has reconciled us into the divine image through Jesus Christ. Therefore, God has passed on to us this ministry of reconciliation that it may be a gift to all peoples, all nations, and all times. We are ambassadors for Christ, and God is making the appeal of reconciliation through us to all the world. We entreat you, therefore, be reconciled constantly to God and to one another. For Christ, who did not know flesh, was made flesh for our sake and for the sake of the world that we might be enfolded into the very righteousness and goodness of God.

Intercessions

In Christ, God has reconciled the whole world in goodness, charity, and peace. That we may be ambassadors of God's unconditional love to all people, we pray: Hear and answer, tender God.

- For all Christians, that without judgment we may bear God's all-powerful love and acceptance to every living creature, let us pray . . .
- For those who suffer from despair fearing an unworthiness that keeps them distant from God's grace and the communion of believers, let us pray . . .
- For the gift of courage that allows us to gaze fully into the mirrored lives of those who seek us out, and that with them we may be faithful and loving companions, let us pray . . .
- For the members of the lesbigay community, that our fear-touched lives may be a source of blessing and grace for those who are searching for human love and communion, let us pray . . .
- And for our individual needs . . . , let us pray . . .

Closing

O God, you do not desire your people to be lonely, but wish us to share the bread and cup of human communion with one another. Look upon your people. See those who are caught in the grip of despair and fear. In Christ, break their chains and teach us always to serve their needs as we would our own with courage and grace. We ask this, as all things, through Christ in the unity of the Holy Spirit, with you, one God, forever and ever. Amen.

The Lord's Prayer. Abba in heaven, your name is holy! Your justice come, your will be done, on earth as in the heavens. Fill us this day with all that we need. Teach us to heal as you have healed us. Bring us not to the test, but deliver us always from the power of evil. You alone are God, and all belongs to you!

4
As Bread That Is Broken

Presence | Recall the loving presence of God.

Reflection | In recent decades, church tradition has reclaimed the relationship between our celebration of the Eucharist and our service of poor and dispossessed people. There is nothing novel about this relationship. Paul roundly criticized the wealthy members of the Corinthian community for choosing the prime places at table and bringing fine food to the Lord's Supper and then not sharing it. In remarkably strong language, Paul declared that such discrimination and selfishness committed within the Eucharist were a blatant contradiction, if not a sacrilege.

In many Christian communities, the weekly celebration of the Eucharist, or Holy Communion, is seen as essential. We remember Jesus the Christ every time we break the bread and share the cup. But the acts of breaking and sharing, of eating and drinking, are specifically meant to nourish us for the breaking open and sharing of our life and goods, giving food and drink and love to those who are hungry and thirsty. Christ enjoins each of us to make a preferential option for service to the poor.

On the journey from exile to freedom, preoccupation with our own needs may tempt us to avoid the call to service. Yet in faith, we know that we are called to make a difference for all our sisters and brothers. Without putting aside our work to achieve justice and peace for our community, lesbigays are called likewise to work for the needs of all people who are poor, needy, dispossessed, and lonely. As with all Christians, our experiences in life are meant to be a springboard for our participation in the broader needs of social justice. When we break our bread for all others in our world, our compassion and strength of service become a leaven in the one loaf that is the Body of Christ.

Soupline

Two hollowed pools framed within the vapors of the kitchen
    air
gazed back at me intensely from the front of the counter.
My hair seemed to stand on end
as she followed every emotion that was beating in my chest.
A young boy and girl clutched at her scraggy skirt,
a younger child in her arms.
That look,
like God throwing a glance at chariots and warriors,
made me stop dead in my tracks
with the soup ladle suddenly frozen midair in my hand.
For a brief moment time stood still,
my breath stolen by this fearful appearing
of the world at my doorstep.
Such despair.
Not even a hand to knock at the door of my heart.
She just stood there.
Motionless.
Seeming not to move except for the tugging
that hungry children coupled with their whimpering.
She stared at me the kind of stare
that raises guilt from every corner,
the guilt that makes every memory of every meal
seem suddenly distasteful
wanting to be hidden from view.
Caught between acting and not acting,
the earth seemed suspended in its rotation:
the holiday season arrested in its tracks.
This giving suddenly seemed empty of any dignity
like an out-of-place suit in an out-of-place gathering.
Which was worse:
not to feed her
or to make this meal into another act of pity?
I wondered what had made me come here this day.
What could have possessed me?
Anger dried my throat.
I thought I was giving something of my holiday.
I thought that I was acting out of love.
And all that struck me now was something dirty and less
    worthy.
I felt sullied for the money in my pocket,
the clothes upon my own back,
the thought of car and home and friends,
the work world which was mine to enter each working day.

Canticle

Here was no sloucher,
no parasite feeding off my proud taxes.
Here was despair all wrapped in human telling
with children born to pass this sadness down the
      generations.
Her eyelids momentarily closed
without her emptiness ever blinking.
How I wished this could be like the end of a happy story
where the poor before me would smile in recognition
and my guilt might vanish into forgetfulness.
Her empty poverty never blinked, never faltered.
Poverty is like that after all.
It never steps away
but only leaves a deep indelible impression
like the empty hollow eyes before me.
I have no idea how long my hand was frozen in midair.
But a bit of life came back into my fingers.
Quickly, I filled her bowl and those of her children.
I wanted to push some extra crackers into her pockets.
But she turned away and drone-like found a place at the
      tables.
And all I could do was turn away and weep.
But weep for what?
For her?
For her children?
For an unthankful and uncaring world?
For me?
In the end there was only one thing I knew:
I was there
and was crying.

Reading | Matthew 15:29–39

Jesus looked out at the crowd of four thousand. They had
followed him after he had passed along the Sea of Galilee and
went up a mountainside. They were poor and needy. With
them, they brought the sick, the sorrowing, the lame, the
blind, the mute, and many others. All these gathered at
Jesus' feet looking for something. Perhaps they had no idea
what it was for which they were searching. Whatever the
case may be, desperation is what made their feet quicker and
their hearts more open. He laid hands on them. Many were
cured. But Jesus looked out and saw a more stark hunger in
their eyes. The poor always have that look, that hollowness
that comes from years of wanting. Jesus was moved with

compassion and ordered his disciples to give them something to eat. But there was nothing but a few loaves of crusty bread and a couple of fish. How in the world would this crowd be fed? Even more amazing, how would the disciples be able to make such a ragtag crowd to be seated with one another? Jesus calmly lifted his eyes and gave thanks. The bread and fish were broken and given over. And there was enough at the end to fill seven baskets full! Jesus smiled.

Intercessions

God has given us to one another that our love and needs may be fulfilled. That God may strengthen us for the task of feeding one another, we pray: Hear and answer, tender God.
- For all those in our world who are hungry, lonely, and dispossessed, that the Spirit of God may enlighten our mind to discover how we may serve them, let us pray . . .
- For those who serve the poor in the ministries of justice and peace, that their example and their words may not fall upon deaf ears among us, let us pray . . .
- For all who feel no compassion for the poor and the needy, that the gentle Spirit of God may open their heart to share their goods and life with those less fortunate than themselves, let us pray . . .
- For the members of our lesbigay community, that the Spirit of God may move us beyond ourselves to serve the needy and give witness to the boundless nature of God's love in our life, let us pray . . .
- And for our individual needs . . . , let us pray . . .

Closing

O God of bread and wine, when Jesus walked among us you touched the poor and those whom the world counts as nothing. Each day we venture into our world and see the devastation that our selfishness perpetuates. Send forth your spirit. Break the chains of our selfish pride. Move us to open our heart, our home, and our abundance so that the children of your earth may never again go hungry or thirsty. We ask this, as all things, through Christ in the unity of the Holy Spirit, with you, one God, forever and ever. Amen.

The Lord's Prayer. Abba in heaven, your name is holy! Your justice come, your will be done, on earth as in the heavens. Fill us this day with all that we need. Teach us to heal as you have healed us. Bring us not to the test, but deliver us always from the power of evil. You alone are God, and all belongs to you!

5
Until He Comes Again

Presence	Recall the loving presence of God.
Reflection	From the very beginnings of Christianity, the disciples of Jesus have lived in the spirit of Christ's promise to come again. Over the course of the ensuing centuries, Christians have struggled mightily between living in this world and living for the next world. Many of us are well acquainted with the particular difficulties that result from this creative tension. However, contemporary theologians have reminded us that all Christians live essentially within this world, and should do so in such a way that our life heralds, announces, and prepares the world for that time of future fulfillment.

We attempt to discover the answers for our world's difficulties. Yet we realize profoundly that every human discovery, human knowledge itself, is finite. All forms of human progress, in some measure, have failed to bring about complete peace and justice for individuals and nations. Hence, we are rightly reminded from our tradition that something beyond us must inform and guide our life and our values, the Spirit of God alive among us.

Jesus urges us to build the City of God. Every time we nurture God's peace and justice, we announce the Reign of God. All believers, lesbigay disciples included, are called to live and work and witness with the values of Christ guiding us. As we minister here, we keep our eye on the "already but not yet" Reign of God's justice and peace.

Canticle	**Patmos**

I, a writer,
was searching for a new heaven and a new earth.
My former heaven and my former earth
had vanished into the mists of distant memories
a broken promise believed by a heart more broken still

a broken dream now dormant
until some dawning day when everything folds into peace.
I, a writer,
was lonely on a solitary island
robbed of every motivation and every dreaming.
I was searching and did not know for what.
Voices whispered around me:
Strong voices of anger and resentment,
others, screams of taunting laughter—
tempting me to think that I was nothing after all.
This is the life you live on solitary islands
where you wonder if you will always be alone
caught up only with misty memories.
Mists have a way of robbing your soul
and lulling you to believe that truly you are a nothing.
In that moment, when past graces
and a once-thought evanescent peace
were like a bitter aftertaste and reminder,
it takes the gift of silence
to hear new voices and new messages.
It takes the discipline of silence and the craft of rich
        imagination
to anticipate the coming once again
of other heavens and a newer earth.
Silent in the moment
hollowed out and waiting
an inner voice welled up within me
and bid me write again.
This time, it told me, write from city streets
and write from human hearts,
write about the smallest of earth's children
and all the exiles who live on all the islands
at the furthest ends from every nation.
Speak a word to every church.
Speak a word to every human heart.
Write of new heavens and a newer earth
where every wound is bound in joy
and every hunger filled
and every thirst satisfied with justice.
Let the angels speak again to every corner of the world
that dark despair and human hatred
can come to an end
if we let them

if we put aside the weaponry of fear
and dull the sword of every indecision
and make our cause the cause of every human heart
that searches for that final heaven and that final earth
where justice reigns supreme
and peace is the eternal banquet.
And so I took up a pen and wrote,
carving hopeful visions onto paper
about cloud days and fire nights,
and I scribed the words of canticles
for freedom.

Reading | Revelation 22:12–17;20–21

"See I am coming to you again very, very soon. I will bring with me the fullness of life and all rewards. I will crown creation and your lives. I am the beginning and the end. I am the first and the last, the Alpha and the Omega. Blessed are all those who have washed their robes in my life. These have tasted of goodness and truth, and these shall enter into the city of the living. Outside this city are all those who are chained to darkness and oppression and every form of human injustice and falsehood. These are those who have not trusted and cannot trust. It is I, Jesus, the faithful one, the first and the last, who has sent my angels to you with this testimony for all who believe. I am the Root of David, the inheritor of the final Israel. I am like a bright morning star beaming out with light for all the world and for all history. The Spirit and the Bride have joined. They beckon all the nations to enter into the life of heaven. Let anyone who is thirsty drink of the waters of peace and justice and life. Surely I am coming to you very, very soon." And then the disciples of the Lord, hearing these words, continually cry out for all the ages: "Amen. Come Lord Jesus!"

Intercessions | In Christ, God has ushered into our history a final age of justice and peace. That the Spirit of God may fashion our life to proclaim God's Reign in our every word and deed, we pray: Hear and answer, tender God.
- For all Christians, that our life each day may herald the coming of Christ with the fullness of lasting justice and peace, let us pray . . .

- For those whose life and ministry announce the coming of Christ again, that their witness may increase our thirst for God's Reign, let us pray . . .
- For all those who hunger and thirst for righteousness and truth, that our service of their needs may announce the coming of Christ, let us pray . . .
- For lesbigay believers everywhere, that our life and service in our community and throughout the world may give witness to our commitment to Christ who is coming again, let us pray . . .
- And for our individual needs . . . , let us pray . . .

Closing

O God, you promised never to abandon us and to bring us the fullness of your life for the renewal of all creation. When Jesus had completed his revelation of your love for us in the Resurrection, he promised to come again and bring to the whole world the fullness of your justice and peace. Send forth your spirit upon us. Make us faithful and joyful witnesses of your Reign. Despite trials and oppression, keep us strong in your love that our every word and deed may announce your truth for which the whole world is longing. We ask this, as all things, through Christ in the unity of the Holy Spirit, with you, one God, forever and ever. Amen.

The Lord's Prayer. Abba in heaven, your name is holy! Your justice come, your will be done, on earth as in the heavens. Fill us this day with all that we need. Teach us to heal as you have healed us. Bring us not to the test, but deliver us always from the power of evil. You alone are God, and all belongs to you!

Other Books by Edward F. Gabriele

Prayers for Dawn and Dusk

Edward F. Gabriele

"*Prayers for Dawn and Dusk* provides a simple, honest, and nourishing form of daily morning and evening prayer patterned on ancient church tradition. A prayer of adoration, a psalm, petitions of praise, and a closing prayer help one begin the day positively. Thanksgiving, a psalm, intercessions, and a closing prayer end the day gracefully." **Prairie Messenger,** Canada

Although intended primarily for individuals, this book can be used by communities or prayer groups as well. The prayers are short but evocative, and they flow comfortably into meditation.

Paper: ISBN 0-88489-257-3, 6 x 9, 191 pages, $8.95
Spiral: ISBN 0-88489-275-1, 6 x 9, 191 pages, $10.95

Act Justly, Love Tenderly, Walk Humbly
Prayers for Peace and Justice

Edward F. Gabriele

"Gabriele gives a prayerful voice to every social issue. This book is a thesaurus of prayer as well as a grammar of social concerns. For searchers of social justice, the book is a reminder that it is vital to pray for social justice." Tim Unsworth, *National Catholic Reporter*

Paper: ISBN 0-88489-338-3, 6 x 9, 135 pages, $8.95
Spiral: ISBN 0-88489-365-0, 6 x 9, 135 pages, $10.95